INVESTING BASICS

...and

BEYOND

How to approach investing without
getting lost
in the details ...

by Maria Crawford Scott

Editor, *AAII Journal*

AAii

AMERICAN
ASSOCIATION OF
INDIVIDUAL
INVESTORS®

"The American Association of Individual Investors is an independent not-for-profit corporation formed in 1978 for the purpose of assisting individuals in becoming effective managers of their own assets through programs of education, information, and research."

For more information about membership, contact:

American Association of Individual Investors
625 N. Michigan Avenue
Chicago, Ill. 60611
(312) 280-0170, (800) 428-2244
www.aaii.com
ISBN: 1-883328-08-X

CONTENTS

The Big Picture

Pick up almost any investment publication: What are you likely to find? Descriptions of every investment option imaginable, equations for determining stock value, charts depicting future income needs, and a host of other detailed information.

If you are new to the area, these details can be overwhelming. For some, it may stop you in your tracks.

Others of you may plunge in, hoping to learn as you go along.

However, the best approach is to focus first on the overall process. In any complex undertaking, considerable time must be spent on the details. Yet end results are always dependent on how those details fit together. Without an overall approach to guide you, it's easy to get lost in the details and never reach an end result.

THE PROCESS

To give you an overall picture of the overall picture, here's the overall process.

As with any undertaking, it is best to start with the basic principles. The basic investment principles include an understanding of the relationship between risk and return—the trade-off that exists between them, and the various ways that risk can be reduced.

While the investment principles will be discussed in general terms in the beginning to help set the overall framework, these same principles will apply more specifically at every stage of the process. In fact, all investments should be analyzed with these principles in mind.

Next, it is important to understand how personal circumstances affect investment decisions. If these factors made no difference, we could simply publish one suggested portfolio for everyone to follow. However, your tolerance for risk, your return needs (whether income or growth), the length of time you can remain invested, and your tax status all have an important impact on the kinds of investments you should be emphasizing, and the kinds of investments you should avoid.

ASSET ALLOCATION

Your personal investment profile is the start of the asset allocation process, which consists of dividing your portfolio up among the major asset categories of stocks, bonds and cash.

The asset allocation decision is extremely important—the decisions you make here will have a far greater impact on your overall portfolio return than more specific decisions

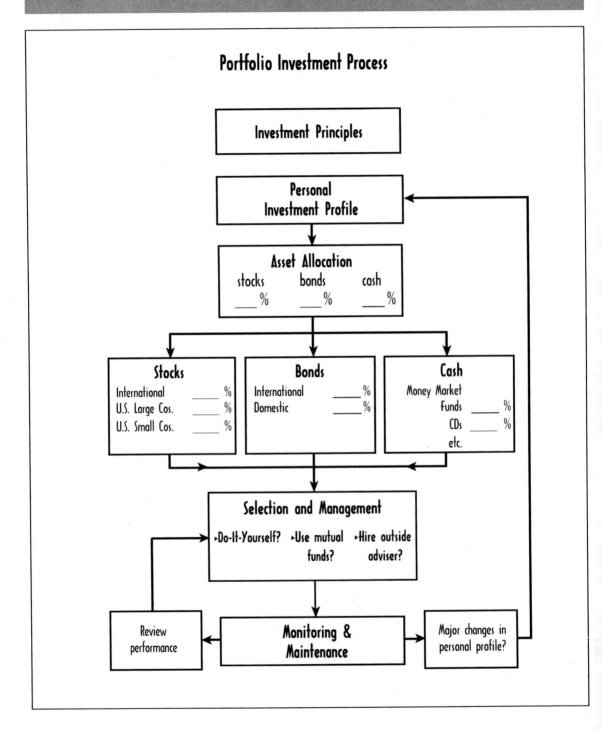

Portfolio Investment Process

Investment Principles

Personal Investment Profile

Asset Allocation

stocks	bonds	cash
____ %	____ %	____ %

Stocks

International	____ %
U.S. Large Cos.	____ %
U.S. Small Cos.	____ %

Bonds

| International | ____ % |
| Domestic | ____ % |

Cash

Money Market	
Funds	____ %
CDs	____ %
etc.	

Selection and Management

‣Do-It-Yourself?   ‣Use mutual funds?   ‣Hire outside adviser?

Review performance

Monitoring & Maintenance

Major changes in personal profile?

assuming, of course, that you stick to the investment principles outlined here.

Next, you will make allocation decisions within the major categories. For instance, your stock portfolio can be divided among large capitalization stocks, small capitalization stocks, and international stocks. Your bond portfolio can be divided into international bonds and domestic bonds, with the latter being further divided among long-term and intermediate-term bonds, high-quality corporates, lower-quality corporates, governments, and municipals. And your cash portion can be divided among such instruments as money market funds and certificates of deposit.

Once these decisions are reached, you will be ready to make selections among the various investment options. Your selections can either be made by an outside adviser (for instance, by hiring a private investment adviser or a financial planner), by investing in mutual funds, or by doing it yourself through individual stock and bond selection.

Lastly, once you have set up your investment portfolio, you must monitor it, making changes when appropriate.

ORGANIZATION OF THE BOOK

The overall portfolio investment process is illustrated on the opposite page. The chapters of this book are structured around this process. This book is designed to provide you with an overall investment approach without losing you to the details, and so it will not discuss more specific topics such as planning for future retirement needs, how to analyze stocks and bonds, how to evaluate mutual funds, etc. Instead, we will provide you with sources for further study if you want to go into more detail. You may also want to read through the book twice: the first time to get the general idea, and the second time to work through the concepts using your own personal profile.

Once you have gone through the process described, you will be well on your way toward successful portfolio investing. The investment principles and your personal investment profile are central to all investment decisions at all levels, and not just to the general investment decisions outlined in this book. An understanding of these basic concepts will help the details seem less overwhelming.

And a clear view of the overall process will keep you focused on your purpose— successful end results for your investment portfolio.

2

The Principles of Investing: Risk, Return, and the Trade-offs

Every builder starts with a foundation. If you are new to investing, you are building an investment portfolio, and you need to start with an investment foundation. That foundation consists of the basic investment principles.

RETURNS AND RISKS

Boiled down to its bare basics, investing concerns returns and risks.

An investor's return consists of current income, plus capital gains due to growth, minus any losses from the investment. Sounds simple, and it is, except that most investors would prefer to know the return before making the investment. Absent a crystal ball, investors can only make an educated guess as to what kind of return to expect. If an investor's actual return turns out to be different than the return he expected, he could suffer an unexpected loss.

Of course, an investor's expected return must be reasonable. Expecting a return of 25% just because your stockbroker says that's what you'll earn is not reasonable. Most expectations are based on what happened in the past, and unfortunately history doesn't always repeat itself. On the other hand, there is little else to go on, and reasonable conclusions about future returns can be reached by looking at the past, tempered with the understanding that these returns aren't guaranteed.

Even if your expectations are reasonable, however, there is the possibility that your investment's actual return will be different than expected. This is the risk you must take on as an investor, and it includes the possibility of losing some or all of your original investment. Risk is greater when the possibility is greater that the actual return will differ from the expected return.

Put another way, *the greater the uncertainty, the greater the risk.*

What is uncertainty? The future is uncertain, and the longer you must wait for your return—or, the longer the time period over which you must make your educated guess as to return—the greater the uncertainty. In addition, the quality and stability of the investment is uncertain. Investors can usually be more certain of their predictions on future returns for investments that have a greater income component because they will receive more of their return sooner rather than later. For instance, bonds that pay a fixed interest rate have more predictable returns than stocks, whose returns come primarily from capital gains.

However, this may be offset by uncertainty over the quality of the income payments—whether they will continue to be paid and how certain it is that they will continue at the expected level. A bond backed by the full faith of the U.S. government is more certain to meet its interest payments and pay back principal than a bond backed by a corporation that may or may not suffer financial difficulties.

Sources of Uncertainty

Investment uncertainty is not knowing what is going to happen to your investment. What could cause it to perform differently than you expected? There are several major sources of uncertainty, or risk, that could produce unexpected returns. They include:

- *Business and industry risk:* The uncertainty of an investment's ability to pay investors income, principal, and any other returns due to a significant fall-off in business (either firm-related or industry-wide) or bankruptcy. A stock, for instance, may fall in value because a firm's earnings have unexpectedly dropped due to bad management calls or an industry-wide slowdown.
- *Inflation risk:* The uncertainty over future inflation rates, which results in uncertainty over the future real (after-inflation) value of your investment. An investment that barely keeps pace with inflation will not be able to grow in real terms, leaving you with only as much purchasing power in the future as you have today.
- *Market risk:* The risk that the general market or economic environment will cause the investment to lose value regardless of the particular security. A stock may drop in value simply because the overall stock market has fallen; this is referred to as stock market risk. A bond doesn't face stock market risk, but it may drop in value due to a rise in interest rates; this is referred to as interest rate risk.
- *Liquidity risk:* The risk of not being able to get out of the investment conveniently at a reasonable price. This can occur for a number of reasons. If the market is volatile, you may be forced to sell at a significant loss if you must sell immediately. Another cause can be an inactive market. For instance, it may be difficult to sell a house simply because there are no buyers.

All investments face each of these risks, but the degree of risk varies greatly. For instance, stocks face much less inflation risk than bonds. Over the last 50 years, bonds have barely kept pace with inflation, while stocks have outpaced inflation by about 8% annually. On the other hand, short-term bonds and money market investments face little liquidity risk, while stocks face a greater liquidity risk, since you may be forced to sell at an inopportune time, suffering a large loss.

The Risk/Return Trade-Off

Ironically, it is uncertainty that creates the potential for higher returns. How? Because of the risk/return trade-off. Every investor wants the highest assured return possible. But as we have seen, returns aren't certain and different investors have varying degrees of uncertainty that they are willing to accept. In fact, each investor seeks the highest possible return at the level of uncertainty, or risk, that he is willing to accept.

In a competitive marketplace, this results in a trade-off: Low levels of uncertainty (low risk) are the most desirable and are therefore associated with low potential returns. High levels of uncertainty (high risk) are the most undesirable and are therefore associated with high potential returns. Over the last 50 years, stocks have produced returns that average 13% annually, long-term bonds have averaged 5% annually, and short-term Treasury bills have averaged 4.5% annually. These returns reflect the risk/return trade-off.

The trade-off, however, exists on average, not in every single instance: Remember, it's the uncertainty that's the risk. As an investor, you must analyze each investment, comparing the potential returns with the risks. On average, the potential returns from an investment should compensate you for the level of risk undertaken. If they do not—for instance, low potential returns associated with high risk—you should not make the investment.

The trade-off also serves as a warning flag—high potential returns usually flag high risks, even when those risks are not obvious at first glance. Remember those higher-yielding certificates of deposit issued by aggressive savings and loans in the 1980s? CD holders unaware of their savings and loan's financial situation who are now trying to collect their guaranteed deposits from the FSLIC would probably re-evaluate their decision if they could do it over again.

Diversification: Reducing Risk

While potential returns should compensate you for risk, there are some risks that you will not be compensated for, and therefore they should be avoided.

If you invest in a single security, your return will depend solely on that security; if that security flops, your entire return will be severely affected. Clearly, held by itself, the single security is highly risky. If you add nine other unrelated securities to that single security portfolio, the possible outcome changes—if that security flops, your entire return won't be as badly hurt. By diversifying your investments among 10 securities, you have substantially reduced the risk of the single security. However, that security's return will be the same whether held in isolation or in a portfolio.

Lower risk, similar return, better investment.

Diversification substantially reduces your risk with little impact on potential returns. The key involves investing in categories or securities that are dissimilar: Their returns are affected by different factors and they face different kinds of risks.

Diversification should occur at all levels of investing. Diversification among the major asset categories—stocks, fixed-income and money market investments—can help reduce market risk, inflation risk and liquidity risk, since these categories are affected by different market and economic factors. Diversification within the major asset categories—for instance, among the various kinds of stocks (international or domestic, for instance) or fixed-income products—can help further reduce market and inflation risk. And as shown in the 10-security portfolio, diversification among individual securities helps reduce business risk.

The importance of diversification can be seen by restating it in the negative: If you don't diversify, you are taking on a considerable risk for which you will not be compensated.

TIME DIVERSIFICATION

There is one other type of diversification that is extremely important yet often overlooked—time diversification, remaining invested over different market cycles.

Time diversification helps reduce the risk that you may enter or leave a particular investment or category at a bad time in the economic cycle. It has much more of an impact on investments that have a high degree of volatility, such as stocks, where prices can fluctuate over the short term. Longer time periods smooth those fluctuations. Conversely, if an investor cannot remain invested in a volatile investment over relatively long time periods, those investments should be avoided. Time diversification is less important for relatively stable investments, such as certificates of deposit, money market funds and short-term bonds.

The best example of the benefits of time diversification is in the stock market. During the infamous month of October 1987, the stock market suffered a loss of over 20%. But do you remember the return for the entire year? If you had invested at the beginning of 1987 and remained invested through year-end, you would have earned 5.2%, not stellar, but certainly better than a loss of 20%. Longer time periods illustrate the point further. For instance, over the five-year period from 1987 through 1991, which includes the market crash, you would have earned an average 15.4% annually if you had remained fully invested in the market, with actual annual returns varying between –3.2% in 1990 and 30.5% in 1991.

Time diversification also comes into play when investing or withdrawing large sums of money. In general, it is better to do so gradually over time, rather than all at once, to reduce risk.

THE BASE

The foundation of your investment portfolio rests on the investment principles of risk and return:

- Returns are not known in advance. Instead, investors must make their decisions using return expectations, which should be reasonable and mesh with reality.

- All investments are made with the possibility that your actual return won't meet your expectations.
- The uncertainty surrounding the actual outcome of your investment creates risk; the greater the uncertainty, the greater the risk.
- There are many reasons why your expectations may not materialize, and you should be aware of all of them, including: business or industry risk, inflation risk, liquidity risk, and market risk. All investments face each of these risks, but to varying degrees.
- There is a trade-off between risk and potential return: the higher the potential returns, the greater the risk; and the lower the potential returns, the lower the risks. Conversely, be wary of claims of high returns with low risk.
- In a portfolio, some risks can be reduced or eliminated with little effect on return through diversification. Always diversify among asset categories (stocks, bonds, cash), within asset categories, and among individual securities.
- Diversification is also important across market environments—the longer your holding period, the better. Don't invest in stocks or other volatile investments if you will remain invested for less than five years.
- Do not take on risks for which you will not be compensated.

In building your investment portfolio, you will be seeking answers to these questions:

- What are the risks?
- What risks can be eliminated or reduced through diversification and which risks will remain?
- What are the returns associated with the risks I will be undertaking?

The answer to the last question will be a balance of those risks and potential returns based on your investment profile—your personal circumstances and personal tolerance for risk. Once you have gained your balance and have a steady foundation, you can finish building your portfolio.

3

Investment Decisions and Your Personal Investment Profile

Investing would be easy if one master investment plan could be followed by all individual investors.

However, no two investors are alike either in terms of personality or in their own financial situations. A master plan simply will not meet your individual needs. Instead, it is necessary for you to tailor your investment plan based on your own personal investment profile. To do that, you need to understand how the various aspects of your personal profile can affect investment decisions.

YOUR PERSONAL INVESTMENT PROFILE

There are four basic aspects that compose your personal investment profile:
- Your personal tolerance for risk;
- Your return needs and whether you need to emphasize current income or future growth;
- Your time horizon; and
- Your tax exposure.

In the last chapter, we discussed risk, return, the trade-off between the two, and the ways risk can be reduced or eliminated with little impact on return. These are the issues upon which all investment decisions are based.

Each aspect of your personal investment profile will affect the trade-offs you are willing to make and your ability to reduce risk.

RISK TOLERANCE

The amount of risk you are willing to take on is an extremely important factor to consider before making an investment because of the severe consequences of taking on too much risk. Risk is uncertainty—the possibility that the investment won't perform as expected. Most investors who take on too much risk panic when confronted with losses they are unprepared for, and they frequently bail out at the worst possible time. Stock investors who panicked and sold right after a stock market crash moved out of the market at one of its lowest points. The result—buying high and selling low—is the opposite of Will

Rogers' famed investment advice, and is guaranteed to produce an unhappy outcome. Properly assessing your tolerance for risk is designed to prevent you from making panic decisions, abandoning your investment plan mid-stream at the worst possible time. How can tolerance be measured?

While many questionnaires seek to grade risk tolerance, the best approach is to simply examine the worst-case scenario—a loss over a one-year period—and ask yourself whether you could stick with your investment plan in the face of such a loss.

Investors with a low tolerance for risk generally can sustain losses of no more than 5% over a one-year period. Individual securities with this kind of characteristic include money market funds and certificates of deposit, both of which protect the underlying principal investment with virtually no risk of loss, and short-term bond investments.

Investors with a moderate tolerance for risk can generally withstand losses of between 6% to 15% over a one-year period. Types of securities that may sustain these kinds of losses include intermediate- and long-term bond portfolios and high-quality, lower-risk dividend-paying stock portfolios.

Investors with a high tolerance for risk can generally withstand losses of between 16% to 25% annually. Security types that may sustain these kinds of losses include aggressive growth stock portfolios, portfolios of stocks of smaller firms, and emerging market stock portfolios.

Note that in the "Personal Investment Profile" table presented later in this chapter, the examples of security types are presented merely to give you an idea of the level of losses discussed. If you are drawn to one of those kinds of securities, you probably have a tolerance for risk approaching that type of security. The examples are not meant to limit investors solely to the choices within each risk level. In fact, we shall see later that even a low-risk investor can benefit by diversifying into riskier investments with part of their portfolio while maintaining a low-risk profile. In addition, the losses outlined are typical for the security types as a group; individual securities within these types could sustain losses much greater than a portfolio of securities.

RETURN NEEDS

Individuals differ greatly in their return needs. If you depend on your investment portfolio for part of your annual income, for example, you will want returns that emphasize relatively higher annual payouts that tend to be consistent each year and protect principal.

On the other hand, individuals who are saving for a future event—a child's education, a house, or retirement, for instance—would want returns that tend to emphasize growth. Of course, many individuals may want a blending of the two—some current income, but also some growth.

Determining your return needs is important because you can't have all of everything— there is no investment that offers a high certain payout each year, protects your principal *and* offers a high potential for future growth.

There are a number of trade-offs here, based on the risk/return trade-off. First, the price for principal protection is lower returns, usually in the form of lower annual income. There is also a trade-off between income and growth: The more certain the annual payment, the less risky the investment, and therefore the lower the potential return in the form of growth.

These trade-offs can be seen by looking at examples of individual securities from least risky to most risky:

- Money market funds, certificates of deposit and short-term bonds offer the most certain annual payouts plus protection of principal, but offer virtually no potential for growth.
- Longer-term bonds offer higher annual payouts, but less protection of principal and little growth potential.
- High-quality dividend-paying stocks offer less certain annual payouts, since dividends aren't assured, and no principal protection since stock prices aren't guaranteed, but they offer considerable growth potential.
- Finally, growth stocks offer the most potential for growth but rarely pay dividends.

Again, these securities are mentioned only as examples of return characteristics to help you identify your own needs. Individuals with specific return needs will not necessarily invest exclusively in securities with those same characteristics. Diversifying among different types of securities in the proper proportion will still allow you to meet your return needs, as long as you have identified them properly.

TIME HORIZON

The length of time you will or can be invested is important because it can directly affect your ability to reduce risk.

In the last chapter, we discussed time diversification—remaining invested through various market cycles. Time diversification is most critical for volatile investments such as stocks, where prices fluctuate greatly over the short term, but are considerably smoothed over longer time periods.

If your time horizon is short, you cannot effectively be diversified across different market environments. Longer time horizons allow you to take on greater risks—with a greater return potential—because some of that risk can be reduced through time diversification.

How should time horizon be measured? Your time horizon starts whenever your investment portfolio is implemented and ends when you will need to take the money out of your investment portfolio. If you are investing to save for a specific event, such as tuition payments or the purchase of a house, your time horizon is fairly easily measured—it ends when you need the cash.

If you are investing to accumulate a sum for periodic withdrawals, such as during retirement, your time horizon is more difficult to quantify as you approach the time that withdrawals will begin. For instance, when you retire, you may need to take out only part of your investment portfolio as income each year. Your time horizon will be a blend—partly short-term and partly intermediate- or longer-term.

What constitutes short-, intermediate- and long-term horizons?

Time diversification is directly affected by time horizon, so it makes sense to use that as a starting point. To diversify over various economic cycles, you must be invested through one complete economic cycle at the very least. In general, the economic cycle lasts about five years, which can be considered a long-term horizon. An even longer-term horizon—over 10 years—would cover several cycles and ensure even greater time diversification.

What about short- and intermediate-term horizons?

Since these horizons are less than five years, stocks shouldn't be considered. In addition, the sooner you need the investment, the greater the need for principal protection and ease of selling. The time horizon—under five years—effectively limits you to fixed-income securities. If you need the money within a year or two, you are limited to the shorter end of the fixed-income spectrum—money market funds, very short-term bonds and short-term certificates of deposit. An intermediate-term outlook—two to five years—allows you a little more room to earn higher returns using intermediate-term (less than five years) bonds and intermediate-term certificates of deposit.

TAX EXPOSURE

The bottom line to all investors is what's left after taxes. The level at which you are taxed will have a big impact on the kinds of investments that will provide you with the best aftertax return.

Investors who are in higher income tax brackets need to be concerned with the tax implications of their investments. For instance, part of the return from a high dividend-paying stock is in the form of an annual dividend that is taxed each year. High tax exposure investors would want to avoid or shelter in a tax-exempt account, such as an IRA, investments that generate high annual income, and stress those that offer long-term growth, where taxes can be deferred until the investment is sold. If these investors need fixed-income securities, they would probably prefer those that offer some tax exemption, such as municipal securities.

Investors who are in lower income tax brackets need to worry less about the tax implications of their investments. Conversely, they should avoid securities that benefit high tax-exposure investors. For instance, the yields paid on municipal securities are usually attractive only for investors in the top tax brackets.

With the tax laws changing regularly, it is difficult to quantify what constitutes "lower" and "higher" tax exposure (perhaps the terms "high" and "even higher" would be more accurate). However, if your annual income level puts you within the top federal income tax categories, you fall within the "higher" category, and if your income level puts you in the lower federal tax categories, you are in the "lower" category.

The Personal Investment Profile

	Range	Security Groups With These Characteristics
Risk Tolerance How much of a loss can you stomach over a one-year period without abandoning your investment plan?	► Low: 0% to 5% loss ► Moderate: 6% to 15% loss ► High: 16% to 25% loss	► Low: Money market funds, CDs ► Moderate: Intermediate and long-term bonds, conservative high dividend-paying stocks ► High: Growth stocks
Return Needs What form of portfolio return do you need to emphasize: income, growth or both?	► Income: Steady source of annual income ► Growth/Income: Some steady annual income, but some growth is also needed ► Growth: Growth to assure real (after inflation) increase in portfolio value	► Income: Bonds ► Growth/Income: Dividend-paying stocks ► Growth: Growth stocks
Time Horizon How soon do you need to take the money out of your investment portfolio?	► Short: 1 to 5 years ► Long: Over 5 years	► Short: Money market funds, CDs, short-term bonds; intermediate-term bonds (less than 5 years) ► Long: Growth stocks, aggressive stocks
Tax Exposure Based on your annual income, at what bracket will additional income from portfolio earnings and gains be taxed?	► Lower: Annual income is such that marginal tax bracket is among lower rates ► Higher: Annual income is such that marginal tax bracket is among higher rates	► Higher tax exposure securities (stressed by lower tax-exposure investors): Fixed-income securities, high dividend-paying stocks ► Lower tax exposure securities (stressed by high tax-exposure investors): Municipal bonds, non-dividend paying growth stocks

Life Cycle Investing

Your personal investment profile will change over time. For instance, your tolerance for risk may change as you get older, or as you acquire more assets and become more financially secure. When you approach retirement, your time horizon may shift, and become a blend of long-term and intermediate- or short-term needs. As it does so, you will need to make revisions to your investment plan to reflect these changes.

The table below shows how an investor's profile may change over time. The table also illustrates the degree to which profiles can vary.

Of course, your own profile may be very different than the one presented here; your profile may even fit one of those listed here, such as early retirement, even though you are in a different stage—perhaps early career. The table is only an example.

An effective investment portfolio is one that is based on a balance between the risks you are willing to take and the returns you need to achieve your goals. An understanding of the various aspects of your investment profile will allow you to assess that proper balance.

The next step is to match the investment characteristics of the various asset categories to your risk and return characteristics in an efficient manner that maximizes return while minimizing risk.

Life Cycle Investing: A Changing Profile

	Early Career	Middle Career	Late Career	Early Retirement	Late Retirement
Risk Tolerance	High	High	Moderate	Moderate	Low
Return Needs	Growth	Growth	Growth	Growth/Income	Income
Time Horizon	Long	Long	Long	Short/Long	Short/Long
Tax Exposure	Lower	Higher	Higher	Lower	Lower

4

Asset Allocation Among the Three Major Categories

At first glance, many investors assume that the basic asset allocation decision is easy. After all, at this level you are focusing on only three choices—stocks, bonds, and cash (money market funds and short-term certificates of deposit).

While the choices are few, the way you allocate your portfolio among these three categories will have by far the greatest impact on your performance of any investment decision you make, assuming that you don't violate the basic investment principles.

Why? If you follow basic investment principles—and in particular are well-diversified within each category—you will eliminate many of the specific risk characteristics that are unique to a single investment. Most of what will remain, however, are the broad risk and return characteristics of the overall category. For instance, assuming you have a well-diversified stock portfolio of, say, 20 stocks, your decision several years ago to invest in IBM instead of Intel may have caused you to kick yourself once or twice, but it will have cost you far less than a decision several years ago to invest only 10% of your total portfolio in the stock market and the remainder in cash investments.

How does an investor make this important decision?

You should start with one of the basic investment principles: "In building an investment portfolio, you are seeking answers to these questions: What are the risks? What risks can be eliminated or reduced through diversification and which risks will remain? What are the returns associated with the risks I will be undertaking?"

This chapter will try to provide you with an answer to those questions by looking at the historical returns associated with the three major categories. Then, it will show you ways to balance those risks and potential returns based on your personal investment profile.

RISKS AND POTENTIAL RETURNS

Most investors don't possess reliable crystal balls, which makes the future unknown and therefore uncertain. The past, however, is known, and can serve as a useful guide, which we will use here. But there are limitations.

First and foremost, the past may not be repeated.

Second, it is important to look over enough of the past to cover various economic and market conditions, yet to avoid extending so far back that you are viewing conditions that may no longer be applicable due to structural changes in the economy. It is a judgment call, and the data presented in the opposite table covers 1946 through 1996—the post-World War II period.

Lastly, it is important to understand the data itself. The stock data presented here covers the Standard & Poor's 500, which consists of larger, established companies. The bond data is for intermediate-term government bonds, with a maturity of about five years. Cash is represented by Treasury bills, the most conservative segment of the cash investment market. This data represents the core areas in which most investors will concentrate, but there are more volatile segments of each category—small stocks and longer-term bonds, for instance.

The data includes annual returns for the overall period, as well as annual returns based on one-, five-, 10-, 15-, and 20-year holding periods, to indicate how the risk-return equation can change with time. (These holding period returns encompass all the years using rolling holding periods. For instance, five-year periods include 1946 through 1950; 1947 through 1951; etc.). The data also indicates the percentage of holding period returns that were losses, and the percentage of holding period returns that were below the rate of inflation.

In an earlier chapter, the primary investment risks identified were: business and industry risk; market risk; inflation risk; and liquidity risk. Using the historical data, you can start to get an idea concerning the risks and potential returns of the three major categories.

Business and industry risk: At this level, you don't need to focus on business and industry risk because it can be eliminated by diversifying within each category. For instance, within the stock segment, business and industry risk can be eliminated by diversifying among different stocks within different industry groups. However, don't forget this risk at the later stages—it will be a major concern.

Market risk: Both stocks and bonds face substantial market risk—a rise or fall in the value of the investment due to market conditions. A good indication of market risk is to simply examine the best and worst returns over one-year holding periods. Those returns were the kinds of variations that may occur within that category.

Stock market risk is due to the volatility of the overall market, which can cause even attractive stocks to drop in price. For one-year holding periods, stock returns were extremely volatile (and therefore uncertain)—ranging from a high of 52.6% to a low of −26.5%, a substantial loss. In addition, 27% of the one-year holding periods' returns have been losses. Stock market risk does decrease with longer holding periods, as the long-term growth benefits kick in.

Bonds also face substantial market risk due to fluctuating interest rates; this risk is referred to as interest rate risk. Rising interest rates cause existing bonds to drop in value, while falling interest rates cause existing bonds to rise in value; the effect is greater the longer the maturity of the bond. Interest rate risk has caused intermediate-term bond returns to range between 29.1% and −5.1% for one-year holding periods, and suffer losses 11% of the time for one-year holding periods. Interest rate risk decreases only slightly as the holding period increases.

Stock, Bonds and Cash: 1946 through 1996

Returns, Growth, and Income for Entire Period

	Stocks	Bonds	Cash
Average Annual Return (%)	12.1	5.8	4.8
Average Annual Return After Inflation (%)	7.8	1.5	0.5
Average Annual Growth (%)	7.6	0.0	0.0
Average Annual Income (%)	4.5	5.8	4.8

Returns (Annualized) and Losses Based on Holding Period

One-Year Holding Periods	Stocks	Bonds	Cash
Best Return (%)	52.6	29.1	14.7
Worst Return (%)	−26.5	−5.1	0.4
Percentage of Losses (%)	26.8	11.0	0.0
Percentage of Returns Below Inflation (%)	36.6	56.1	36.6

Five-Year Holding Periods			
Best Return (%)	23.9	17.0	11.1
Worst Return (%)	−2.4	1.0	0.8
Percentage of Losses (%)	4.2	0.0	0.0
Percentage of Returns Below Inflation (%)	17.0	29.8	27.7

Ten-Year Holding Periods			
Best Return (%)	20.1	13.1	9.2
Worst Return (%)	1.2	1.3	1.1
Percentage of Losses (%)	0.0	0.0	0.0
Percentage of Returns Below Inflation (%)	14.9	23.4	27.7

Twenty-Year Holding Periods			
Best Return (%)	14.9	9.8	7.7
Worst Return (%)	6.5	2.2	2.0
Percentage of Losses (%)	0.0	0.0	0.0
Percentage of Returns Below Inflation (%)	0.0	11.0	4.0

Stocks: Standard & Poor's 500
Bonds: Intermediate-Term (5-Year) Government Bonds
Cash: Treasury Bills
Source: "Stocks, Bonds, Bills and Inflation—1997 Yearbook," Ibbotson Associates, Chicago.

Cash investments face no market risk because their return is solely based on their current yield.

Inflation risk: All investments face inflation risk—the risk that inflation will erode the real value of the investment. There are two good indications of inflation risk: an investment's real return (its return after inflation) and the percentage of holding period returns that are below inflation.

Stocks face the least inflation risk. Over the entire period, they have produced an annual real return of 7.8%. In contrast, bonds have outpaced inflation by only 1.5% annually, and cash by only 0.5%. Individual holding period returns also indicate the substantial inflation risk facing bond investments. For one-year holding periods, bond returns were below inflation fully 56% of the time; for longer holding periods, inflation risk was similar for bonds and cash; stocks suffered the least.

Liquidity risk: There are two kinds of liquidity risk facing investors. The first is an illiquid market—the inability to sell because of a lack of buyers. Real estate presents the best example: Houses may be on the market for months before a willing buyer appears. For the basic segments of the three investment categories, the markets are quite liquid— there are always willing buyers. The second kind of liquidity risk, however, is that you may be forced to sell at an inopportune time. For instance, if you must sell stocks to raise cash, you may be forced to do so when the market is low. The best indication of this risk

Risk and the Three Major Asset Categories

	Stocks	Bonds	Cash
Business/ Industry Risk	High Can be eliminated through diversification	High (for corp. bonds) Can be eliminated through diversification	None
Stock Market/ Interest Rate Risk	High Return variation: −26.5% to 52.6%	High Return variation: −5.1% to 29.1%	None
Inflation Risk	Low Real average return: 7.8%	High Real average return: 1.5%	High Real average return: 0.5%
Liquidity Risk	Liquid markets but high risk of selling at a loss	Liquid markets but high risk of selling at a loss	Low: Use to reduce liquidity risk of total portfolio

for each category is to examine that category's worst return for a one-year holding period. In addition, you can reduce liquidity risk overall by investing a portion of your portfolio in cash, which doesn't face liquidity risk, lessening the chance that you must sell other investments in bad markets.

Your Personal Investment Profile

Up to this point, the risks and return potentials of the three categories have been viewed individually. However, the most efficient investment portfolios are based on an overall approach that examines the risks and return potential of your total portfolio, not just the individual parts. Diversifying among the asset categories reduces the individual category risks and allows you to build a portfolio that matches your investment profile.

Your investment profile includes your tolerance for risk; your return needs, whether long-term real growth or income; your time horizon; and your tax exposure.

How can you analyze the risk and return potential of a portfolio? To start, the historical data is used here as one possible guide, with the qualification that the future may vary.

Risk tolerance: Use the worst-case scenario—the maximum loss for all categories—as a guide to how much of a loss you can stomach. In the examples here, the worst one-year holding period returns are used.

Return needs: The average annual returns for the entire period, average annual growth and the average income figures can be used to help assess your growth and annual income needs, but keep in mind they are long-term figures; variations year-to-year can be significant.

Bonds and cash produce a steadier source of income than do stocks; a much larger percentage of their annual return comes from income rather than growth. Cash has the advantage of immediate liquidity, but the disadvantage of lower levels of income.

Don't rule out stocks entirely when considering income needs. Dividend income is usually lower than bond income at any given point in time, and dividends are also less assured than bond yields, but the long-term average is not unattractive. Also, it isn't necessary to rely on an income component if you need annual income. You could instead invest for maximum total return, keep a portion in cash for liquidity, and sell stock when necessary.

Stocks clearly are a better source of growth, as well as having the ability to substantially outpace inflation.

Time horizon: The various holding period returns indicate the kinds of risk you face based on your own time horizon. If you are investing only for a short time period, you should not be invested in the stock market, given the substantial losses historically.

On the other hand, the risk/return equation increasingly favors stocks over longer holding periods. Historically, the worst returns for stocks substantially improved the longer the holding period, while for bonds and cash it remained roughly similar. For 20-year holding periods, the worst return for stocks—6.5%—was not much lower than the *best* return for cash over that period, and was considerably higher than the worst return for either bonds or cash.

Tax Exposure: Taxes will hurt your bottom line returns, but there are ways to reduce their impact based on how much you can shelter through tax-exempt accounts (such as IRAs) and specific types of investments (such as municipal bonds). At this stage, however, don't worry about them; this will be covered in Chapter 9.

PUTTING IT TOGETHER

The next step is to examine various possible portfolio combinations to see how they might fit your personal investment profile. Use the risk and return characteristics of the individual categories to help you decide what to emphasize. Then examine the risk and return characteristics of the total portfolio.

The approach is illustrated in the table below, which presents three portfolios representing different asset allocations, along with returns, growth, income, and downside risk.

The figures were derived based on the historical data and the percentage allocated to each category. For instance, the average annual return for Portfolio 1, based on an allocation of 80% stocks and 20% cash, is: [80% × 12.1] + [20% × 4.8] = 10.6%. The downside risk is based on the worst one-year holding period returns for stocks and bonds, and a 0% return for cash (although cash investments always yield positive amounts).

Portfolio 1 is heavily invested in stocks, which indicates that this is a long-term investor with a primary need for long-term growth that outweighs the short-term stock market

Asset Allocation: Three Portfolios

	Average Annual Return (%)	Average Annual Growth (%)	Average Annual Income (%)	Downside Risk (%)*
Portfolio 1: 80% stocks, 20% cash	10.6	6.0	4.6	−21.2
Portfolio 2: 60% stocks, 20% bonds, 20% cash	9.4	4.6	4.8	−16.9
Portfolio 3: 40% stocks, 40% bonds, 20% cash	8.1	3.0	5.1	−12.6

* Based on worst returns for one-year holding periods for stocks and bonds, and 0% for cash.
All figures are based on historical data; future variation can be expected.

Formulas for Determining Your Own Portfolio Profile

Avg. annual return (%): _____ = [_____ × 12.1] + [_____ × 5.8] + [_____ × 4.8]
                                      % in stocks   % in bonds   % in cash

Avg. annual growth (%): _____ = [_____ × 7.6] + [_____ × 0.0] + [_____ × 0.0]
                                      % in stocks   % in bonds   % in cash

Avg. annual income (%): _____ = [_____ × 4.5] + [_____ × 5.8] + [_____ × 4.8]
                                      % in stocks   % in bonds   % in cash

Downside risk (%): _____ = [_____ × –26.5] + [_____ × –5.1] + [_____ × 0.0]
                                 % in stocks   % in bonds   % in cash

risk considerations. The overall characteristics of the portfolio reflect the investor's profile: a high tolerance for risk (the downside risk is –21.2%); less emphasis on annual income; and a higher growth return. This portfolio tends to match the characteristics of many individuals in their early- or mid-career stages of the life cycle, as outlined in the previous chapter.

Portfolio 2 offers a more moderate-risk approach, with a downside risk of –16.9%. The trade-off is lower growth.

Portfolio 3 stresses a higher annual income and lower downside risk. The trade-off, again, is a considerably lower growth. This portfolio tends to match the characteristics of many individuals in retirement.

There are many combinations that can match an individual's profile, and everyone's profile differs. The three portfolios presented here are examples to illustrate the approach. The table above presents formulas you can use to analyze various combinations yourself, using the historical data. Although the historical data was used as a guide, you should use your own judgment as well. For instance, bear market returns could be used for worst-case scenarios, or recent bond and dividend yields could be used for potential income.

In addition, keep in mind that at this stage, the allocation process is a rough guide. Don't spend time agonizing over the difference between a 62.5%/37.5% versus a 60.8%/39.2% stock/cash allocation.

With a rough idea of your overall asset allocation, you can start to refine your selections.

5

Asset Allocation Among the Major Market Segments

Once you have decided on your portfolio allocation among the three major asset categories—stocks, bonds, and cash—your most important work is over. Yet, your portfolio at this point is only broadly sketched. It is now time to rough in a few details.

In the last chapter, the major risks facing the three asset categories were discussed:

- *Business and industry risk* is high for both stocks and bonds, but can be eliminated by diversifying among different stocks with different industry groups;
- *Inflation risk* for bonds is high, but can be reduced by including stocks in the overall portfolio;
- *Liquidity risk* is high for stocks and bonds, but within an investor's portfolio it can be reduced by including cash (money market and short-term certificates of deposit).

That leaves stock market and interest rate risk as the major risks facing investors who diversify their portfolios among the three major asset categories. Stock market risk is due to the volatility of the overall market, which can cause even attractive stocks to drop in price. Interest rate risk is due to the sensitivity of bond prices to changes in interest rates—rising interest rates cause existing bonds to drop in value.

At this stage in the allocation process, the goal is to try either to reduce those risks without substantially affecting overall return, or to enhance return without substantially adding to those risks—or both.

The best approach to reducing stock market and interest rate risks is to find segments within the stock and bond markets that are affected by different kinds of factors. While one segment of the market may be down, the other segment may be less affected, providing higher returns over that period. As we shall see, some of these market segments are much more volatile than the others, but offer a higher return potential. The least volatile segment should be used as the core, with the other segments added to varying degrees depending on your tolerance for risk.

The overall effect of combining these segments is to smooth return variations—and less variation means less risk—without reducing return.

The data used to illustrate these market segments is based on average returns for mutual funds that tend to invest in each market segment. This data is the most meaningful source for comparing market segments for individual investors. However, it only covers a recent and limited time period. The year-by-year returns will provide you with some indication of how the market segments act relative to each other, but you should not assume that the absolute returns in each segment will recur.

THE STOCK MARKET

The largest segment of the stock market (measured by market capitalization—share price times number of shares outstanding) consists of large, well-established companies. The Standard & Poor's 500 usually defines this group; it represents about 70% of the U.S. stock market. Most of these companies are well-known names: IBM, Ford, and AT&T, for instance. The stocks of these firms offer good growth potential, since they grow as the economy expands. They also offer some income, since they tend to pay cash dividends. These companies should form the core of every investor's stock portfolio.

There are two other stock market segments, however, that should not be ignored: small company stocks and foreign firms.

The stocks of smaller U.S. companies in general have a greater potential for long-term growth than large, well-established companies.

However, they also have greater risks. In addition to the risks associated with stocks in general, the stocks of smaller firms have these further risks:

- There may be no yearly income stream since they do not tend to pay dividends.
- It can be harder to obtain information about specific firms, making accurate analysis difficult.
- Their returns tend to be much more volatile, with firms more prone to difficulties during economic downturns.
- Because they have a smaller number of shares outstanding, these stocks tend to be less liquid, making buying and selling more difficult.

While smaller company stocks tend to be more volatile than the stocks of larger firms,

Stock Market Segments: Average Fund Returns 1987-1996 (%)

	1996	1995	1994	1993	1992	1991	1990	1989	1988	1987	1987-1996
Growth & Income Funds	20.2	29.9	-1.1	14.2	11.2	28.9	-6.1	23.0	17.5	0.9	13.2
Int'l Stock Funds	15.0	8.9	-3.3	39.8	-3.8	12.8	-9.8	22.6	14.8	12.2	10.1
Small Co. Funds	17.8	28.4	0.7	16.4	15.6	47.1	-6.9	24.1	18.3	-1.8	15.0
Combination Portfolios											
Conservative	19.4	27.7	-1.1	17.0	10.1	29.1	-6.6	23.1	17.3	1.8	13.1
Aggressive	18.7	27.2	-0.6	17.6	11.5	34.6	-6.8	23.4	17.6	1.0	13.6

studies indicate that their average long-term returns have been greater. If you have a long-term horizon, the addition of small stocks to a core portfolio of larger firms can increase your overall stock portfolio return, if you are willing to take on the extra risk of greater return swings year to year.

The other stock market segment consists of the international market—foreign firms located in Japan (the largest foreign market) and Europe and, to a much lesser degree, the emerging markets of Asia and Latin America.

Foreign stocks have these additional risks:

- Currency risk: The risk that changes in the relative value of the dollar and the currency of the country in which the firm is based will affect an investor's return. Currency risk is one reason returns for foreign firms are so volatile.
- Country risk: The risk that political conditions within a country will affect economic conditions.
- Many foreign company stocks offer little or no annual income.

Foreign stocks offer substantial diversification benefits because they tend to be affected by different economic factors than the U.S. markets. The zigs and zags in return in these stocks do not always coincide with those of U.S. stocks.

An example of how these three market segments have behaved since 1987 is presented in the table on the opposite page. The table presents the average returns for three mutual fund categories: Growth and income funds, which tend to invest in the stocks of larger companies (funds that track the S&P 500 are classified in this category); international stock funds, which invest in foreign stocks; and small capitalization stock funds, which invest in smaller firms.

The yearly return figures illustrate the higher risk of foreign and smaller firm stocks— international stock funds had more yearly losses than did growth and income funds, and the losses for both international stock funds and small company stock funds tended to be larger than for growth and income funds. The figures also illustrate the higher potential returns—smaller stock funds and foreign funds each had single-year returns that approached 40%.

The last two rows illustrate the benefits of adding the two market segments to the large company stock portfolio. The first of these two rows shows a conservative combination of the three categories, consisting of 80% invested in growth and income funds, 10% in small stock funds and 10% in international funds. The second shows a more aggressive combination of 50% invested in growth and income funds, 40% in small stock funds, and 10% in international stock funds. There are, of course, an endless array of combinations; these are presented only as examples. The yearly return figures for these two portfolios compared to the individual market segments provide an indication of the benefits of a mixture.

What about the overall returns? The cycles that favor one market segment over another can extend over long time periods. The 1980s and 1990s tended to favor U.S. firms over foreign firms. In hindsight, it is clear that over this time period, an investor with less foreign exposure would have outperformed an investor with more foreign exposure, and an investor with more small company exposure would have outperformed one with less exposure. However, both combination portfolios are less volatile than the two aggressive segments. It is the uncertainty concerning these patterns that creates risk; by diversifying among these various market segments, you are reducing the risk that you will guess the pattern incorrectly.

THE BOND MARKET

The major bond market segment that most investors concentrate on is the high-quality sector: U.S. government bonds, high-grade corporate bonds, and high-grade municipals. These bonds offer the smallest degree of default risk, clearly a major concern to most fixed-income investors who are concerned about yearly income flows. U.S. government bonds offer the most protection against default. However, diversification among high-grade corporate and municipal issuers can substantially reduce default risk among issuers. Municipal issues offer the added benefit of federal tax-free income.

These bonds, however, all face similar interest rate risk. Bond values are tied closely to the level of interest rates: As interest rates rise, the values of bonds fall; as interest rates fall, the values of bonds rise. Thus fluctuations in interest rates will cause the total return on bonds to fluctuate, with long-term bonds fluctuating more than short-term bonds.

Not all segments of the bond market react to interest rate fluctuations in the same manner. While high-quality bonds tend to be highly sensitive to the level of interest rates in the U.S., two other bond market segments are affected by other variables, and thus tend to behave somewhat differently. These two segments are international bonds and high-yield bonds.

The return on a foreign bond, for a U.S. investor, is based on both the local bond market of the issuer and how the currency in which the bond is denominated performs versus the U.S. dollar. Local bond markets, of course, are affected by the country's economic environment. Currency movements are based on a host of economic factors, as well as non-economic factors such as political considerations by both the U.S. and the other major economic forces. While interest rate movements in the U.S. will have an impact on the dollar, the other variables affecting foreign bonds mean that their returns behave somewhat differently than their U.S. counterparts.

These variables, of course, are also a source of extra risk. Thus, in addition to the risks facing bonds in general, foreign bonds face:

- Currency risk, which applies not only to the return but also can affect yearly coupon payments.
- Country risk.

High-yield bonds are usually issued by firms that have an uncertain financial outlook—either they have fallen into deteriorating credit situations, they are emerging growth companies, or they are undergoing corporate restructurings. The issues are rated below investment grade by bond rating agencies.

While the returns of these bonds are affected by interest rates, they are also responsive

Bond Market Segments: Average Fund Returns 1987-1996 (%)

	1996	1995	1994	1993	1992	1991	1990	1989	1988	1987	1987-1996
Corp. Bond Funds	5.0	17.4	-3.0	11.4	8.7	17.8	3.5	9.4	9.3	2.4	8.0
High-Yield Funds	14.8	18.9	-3.0	19.2	15.9	27.6	-4.8	1.2	12.5	1.8	9.9
Int'l Bond Funds	12.9	16.7	-7.1	14.5	4.4	14.6	13.9	4.8	4.2	15.7	9.2
Combination Portfolios											
Conservative	6.8	17.5	-3.4	12.5	9.0	18.5	3.7	8.1	9.1	3.7	8.3
Aggressive	9.4	17.6	-4.0	14.1	9.4	19.5	4.0	6.2	8.8	5.6	8.8

to the overall economic cycle as well as the growth prospects of the issuing firm. Economic downturns cast major shadows on the future prospects for the issuing firms and their ability to pay their debt. Conversely, a strong economy bodes well for the firms and their bonds. This economic impact works in opposition to the interest rate risk they face: rising rates, which are bad for bonds generally, usually accompany a strong economy, which is good for high-yield bonds; falling rates, which are good for bonds overall, usually accompany a weak economy, which is bad for high-yield bonds. In addition, high-yield bonds are less sensitive to changes in interest rates due to the larger coupons received each year.

Additional risks of high-yield bonds:
- Greater risk of loss, particularly during economic downturns.
- Greater business and industry risk (which should be reduced through diversification), since the chance of default is higher.

An example of how these three market segments have behaved since 1987 is presented in the table above. The table presents the average returns for three mutual fund categories: corporate bond funds, which tend to invest in high-quality corporate bonds; high-yield corporate bond funds; and international bond funds.

The yearly return figures illustrate the higher risk of high-yield bonds. The yearly figures also illustrate the degree to which the three segments are independent—for instance, in 1988, when foreign bond funds averaged only 4.2%, corporate bond funds averaged 9.3%, and high-yield bond funds averaged 12.5%. The tables were turned in 1990, when high-yield bonds returned –4.8% and corporate bonds funds averaged 3.5%, while foreign bond funds returned 13.9%.

The last two rows illustrate conservative and aggressive combinations of these three segments. The conservative combination consists of 80% invested in corporate bond funds, 10% in high-yield bonds, and 10% in international bond funds. The aggressive portfolio consists of 50% invested in corporate bond funds, 25% in high-yield bonds and

25% in international bond funds.

What about the overall returns for the period? Foreign bond funds and high-yield bond funds have fared well in recent years, which is reflected in higher, albeit more volatile, returns. In hindsight, the 1990s favored the conservative stock investor, but the aggressive bond investor.

GUIDELINES FOR ALLOCATING WITHIN SEGMENTS

There really are no satisfactory rules for allocating among market segments.

The core segments—large company stocks and high-quality bonds—in general have the risk and return characteristics of the major asset categories. Small stocks have (from 1946 through 1996) produced returns that are about 1.8% greater than large company stocks, almost all from growth rather than income; the worst one-year return was –30.9%. For the other non-core segments, the lack of comparable long-term performance records makes it difficult to come up with any historical guide.

The allocation decision within these market segments depends on your risk profile: your risk tolerance, return needs (growth and income), and time horizon. There are many different combinations that can match an individual's profile, and everyone's profile differs. The final decision must rest on your own judgment and what you are most

Asset Allocation: A Market Segment Summary

Risk and Return Characteristics	Stock Market Segments			Bond Market Segments		
	Large Co.	Small Co.	International	High-Quality	High-Yield	International
Growth Potential	High	Very High	High	Low	Low	Low
Income	Moderate	Low	Low	High	High but variable	High but variable
Downside Risk	High	Very High	Very High	Low	Moderate	Moderate

One Approach to Allocation Within Segments*	Stock Market Segments			Bond Market Segments		
	Large Co.	Small Co.	International	High-Quality	High-Yield	International
	Core	Non-Core	Non-Core	Core	Non-Core	Non-Core
	80% to 50%	10% to 40%	10% to 40%	80% to 50%	10% to 40%	10% to 40%

*The percentages range from conservative to aggressive. They are based on the concept of effectively diversifying portfolios within the asset classes, with variations based on an investor's personal investment profile. However, final allocation decisions should be based on a thorough understanding of the investment categories. Never invest in an area in which you are uncomfortable with the risks or which you do not understand.

Investing Basics ...and Beyond

comfortable with.

Here, however, are some thoughts to consider:

- A core position consists of at least a 50% commitment. For each major asset class, the most conservative segment should serve as a core. Using this approach, at least 50% of a stock portfolio would be invested in the stocks of larger firms, and at least 50% of a bond portfolio would be invested in high-quality bonds (government bonds, high-quality corporates, and high-quality municipals).
- At least 10% of a portfolio must be committed to a market segment to have a meaningful effect. Using this approach, at least 10% of a stock portfolio would be invested in small firm stocks and 10% in foreign stocks, while for a bond portfolio, at least 10% would be invested in high-yield bonds and 10% in foreign bonds. This would also mean that the maximum commitment to each core segment by a conservative investor would be 80% of the stock or bond portfolio. Conservative investors can reduce the risk in the core segment of their bond portfolio even further by shortening its average maturity.
- Given the above limits, commitments to the non-core market segments could range from 10% to 40%, depending on an investor's risk tolerance and preference for a particular market segment. For instance, an aggressive investor who favored smaller stocks over foreign stocks may have a stock portfolio that consists of 50% large firm stocks, 40% small firm stocks and 10% foreign stocks.
- Keep in mind the goal of diversifying among market segments, which is to reduce the major risks of the major asset classes (stock market risk for stocks and interest rate risk for bonds). The various market segments move in different cycles; one may do much better than another over certain time periods. Diversifying reduces the risk that you will guess incorrectly which market segment will do well in the near future.
- Make sure that you take into consideration any income needs. Small stocks and many international stocks don't pay much income; income from high-yield and foreign bonds may be higher than for high-quality bonds, but also more variable.
- Make sure that you understand the added risks of the non-core segments, particularly the downside risk.
- These considerations should never override the most basic investment principle—never invest in anything you don't understand.

The objective at this point in time is to expand on the broad asset categories. Decisions on investment style—for instance, should you invest in value stocks or growth stocks—and on specific stock or bond selections are made at a later stage, after you have decided who will handle the selection decisions.

6

Your Investment Plan: How Will It Be Implemented?

The broad outlines of your portfolio have been drawn, and some of the details have been sketched in. But to implement your decisions, individual securities must be selected and put together in a portfolio for each of your selected categories. The next question is: Are you going to do this all yourself or use some outside expertise, and if you do use outside help, who do you turn to?

Fortunately, the choice isn't necessarily one vs. the other. Most investors will use some outside expertise. The amount and type of outside help you use will depend on your needs, the size of your portfolio, and your own knowledge and expertise.

What kind of expertise should you look for? For the most part, at this stage you are looking for investment management skills, which consist of:

- Portfolio composition expertise: How various securities will be combined (through the use of a proper investment strategy) to construct a portfolio that meets the defined objectives.
- Individual security selection and buy/sell timing expertise: Finding and analyzing the specific securities that will fit into the overall portfolio and making decisions as to when they should be purchased and sold.

THE VARIOUS FINANCIAL EXPERTS

Who has this expertise? There is a wide variety of financial experts that individuals turn to for advice. There is also considerable confusion as to the kind of advice they are best at offering. Not all of these financial advisers are the best choice for seeking outside investment management help.

The following is a run-down of various kinds of financial advisers and the typical functions they perform:

Financial Planners: A financial planner is a generalist who helps individuals delineate financial plans with specific objectives, and helps coordinate various financial concerns, such as savings and investment, insurance, estate planning, and tax planning. Planners will use other experts, such as accountants and attorneys, for more specific advice. Professional designations include the CFP (Certified Financial Planner) and the ChFC

(Chartered Financial Consultant).

Some financial planners receive part or all of their compensation through commissions on investment products they sell, which presents potential conflict-of-interest problems. Planners that charge on a fee-only basis avoid these problems; their charges will vary with the complexity of the plan.

A financial planner will help individuals set up an asset allocation strategy (roughly following the approach outlined in this series) and advise in its implementation, for example by recommending the use of specific mutual funds or investment advisers. Many are registered with the Securities and Exchange Commission (SEC) as registered investment advisers because of the advice they do provide. However, most do not manage investment portfolios—they do not make portfolio composition and individual stock selection decisions—for their clients.

Investment Advisers: An investment adviser, also referred to as a money manager, is someone who manages assets—making portfolio composition and individual security selection decisions—on a fully discretionary basis with a very specific, clearly-defined investment philosophy and strategy.

There are various kinds of advisers, ranging from independent investment advisory firms to bank trust departments. In addition, many brokerage firms have arrangements with certain investment advisers to provide advice to clients through "wrap accounts."

Many advisers will be CFAs (Chartered Financial Analysts), which requires passage of a rigorous series of tests covering portfolio management and individual security selection. Investment advisers are required to register with the SEC as registered investment advisers (RIA), but this only indicates that they have filed the proper form and paid the required fee.

Most advisers charge a percentage of the assets under management (usually a decreasing percentage with larger portfolios) and may have minimum account sizes or charge a flat fee for accounts below a certain size. The best known advisory firms tend to manage institutional accounts—for instance, pension plans and mutual funds—and may have minimums of $1 million or more.

There are many smaller and lesser-known firms, however, that manage assets for individuals. While fees vary considerably, typical charges are 2% to 3% of assets for smaller portfolios, with $100,000 being a typical minimum portfolio size. Portfolios of $500,000 or more may receive reduced rates. Brokerage commissions and custodial fees (if any) are additional.

Charges for brokerage firm wrap accounts, on the other hand, are all-inclusive, with the fee covering both brokerage commissions and the advisory fee. Typical fees range from 2% to 3%, with $100,000 a typical minimum.

Independent investment firms can tailor an individual's portfolio to his needs and circumstances. For instance, purchases and sales of individual securities can be better timed to coincide with an investor's tax planning needs.

While an investment adviser helps with the overall asset allocation strategy, an investor's portfolio is limited to the area of the adviser's expertise. For instance, most smaller advisers concentrate on U.S. stock and bond markets. Because of the large minimums and higher fees associated with smaller portfolios, it would be difficult for most individuals to use more than one adviser to achieve broad diversification among major asset categories.

In addition, comparative information on investment advisers is much more difficult to find. Unlike mutual funds, which are single portfolios where performance evaluation is easily made using information and reports that the funds are required to make public, advisers manage numerous separate portfolios and are not required to make information on those portfolios available to the public. To evaluate potential advisers, investors must do their own research and analyses based on information provided by the adviser, use a brokerage firm's recommendations (through a wrap account), or use the services of a consultant. (Appendix B goes into more detail on selecting an investment adviser.)

Mutual Funds: A mutual fund pools investors' money to invest in securities; the pool is then managed by an investment adviser. Since the pool can become very large and advisory fees are based on portfolio size, mutual funds are able to attract some of the best investment talent as portfolio managers. For individuals, the economies of scale provided by a pooled approach mean that advisory fees are actually quite low; brokerage expenses can also be held down. In addition, minimum account sizes are low, providing access to investors with smaller portfolios. In sum, mutual funds provide individuals with access to extremely good investment management talent at a low cost. They also provide individuals with access to a diversified group of securities that only a large portfolio can provide.

The average expense ratio for no-load stock funds is 1.5%, while for low-load bond funds it is 1%; this does not include brokerage commissions. Minimum initial investments vary; $1,000 is typical, but there are funds that have lower initial minimums. No-load or low-load funds are suggested because a load is simply a sales commission and does not go toward better investment management.

Investors who use no-load or low-load mutual funds must, for the most part, make their own asset allocation decisions, both among the three major asset categories, and within those categories. On the other hand, there are a wide variety of mutual funds, providing investors with access to investment management expertise in such diverse areas as smaller firm stocks, international stocks, international bonds and emerging markets. There are a few "asset allocation" funds that offer diversification among major asset categories.

Finally, there is extensive information available on mutual funds, not only concerning performance but also on their investment strategy, portfolio holdings, turnover, etc.

Stockbrokers: Individual stocks and bonds are sold through stock brokerage firms. As a client of the firm, you work with a stockbroker. Stockbrokers typically undergo a short training course provided by the firm in order to obtain a license to do business through the firm. Once licensed, they become registered representatives, registered with the exchanges and in the various states in which the firm does business.

Stockbrokers with full-service brokerage firms can offer investment advice, as extensive or as little as desired by the client. For the client, there is no additional charge for this advice, and brokers are required to act in the best interest of their customers. However, the potential for a conflict of interest exists since a large part of a full-service broker's compensation is determined by commissions earned on sales of securities and other investment products. In addition, full-service brokerage firms offer brokers different percentage commissions for various products, which gives the broker an incentive to favor certain products over others. To ease some of these concerns, many full-service brokerage firms now offer wrap accounts—portfolio composition and security selection decisions provided by an investment adviser (not a broker) who uses the brokerage firm for the trades.

Stockbrokers at discount brokerage firms are fully licensed but paid by salary, not commissions. While they can provide some information about specific stocks—for instance, recent news concerning a firm—most will not provide security recommendations or portfolio composition advice, although some do.

For investors who are making their own portfolio composition and security selection decisions, brokerage firms can provide useful investment research information on particular companies, and a good broker can be very helpful when advice is needed concerning execution of a particular type of trade. But individuals should not look to brokers as a primary source of investment management expertise.

Do-It-Yourself: Investing on your own requires considerable expertise, but there are special opportunities that knowledgeable investors can exploit. In addition, there is no advisory fee, and the use of discount brokers can keep brokerage fees low. You can also tailor your portfolio more specifically to personal needs and circumstances.

However, there are several practical aspects to consider. The first consideration is the size of your portfolio. Diversification is essential, and studies indicate that at least 10 different stocks are required for adequate diversification.

In addition, 100-share lots involve lower transaction costs. Assuming an average share price of $25 per share, you would need at least $25,000 for your stock portfolio alone to achieve a minimum amount of diversification. Much larger portfolio amounts would be required to achieve adequate diversification among different asset categories.

Similarly, a bond portfolio requires adequate diversification, although you could limit credit risk by investing in federally insured government securities.

Secondly, there are many investment categories where it is simply too difficult for individual investors to obtain the necessary information or expertise—high-yield bond investing and the international markets are good examples.

One useful strategy is to supplement your individual stock portfolio with no-load or low-load mutual funds. The mutual funds would ensure your participation in the overall market, and lend diversification to your portfolio, while the individual securities would provide you with the opportunity to apply your specific investment analysis skills.

COMPARING THE ALTERNATIVES

Outside expertise in investment management is provided mainly by investment advisers and mutual funds, with financial planners providing some help as well. The table below summarizes their areas of expertise, costs, and minimums.

Outside Experts

Expertise provided	Financial Planners	Investment Advisers	Mutual Funds
▸ Coordination with other financial concerns	Yes	No	No
▸ Asset allocation among major categories	Yes	Some	A few funds
▸ Portfolio composition decisions	No	Yes	Yes
▸ Individual security selection and buy/sell timing decisions	No	Yes	Yes
Typical minimums	Varies	$100,000	$1,000
Typical fees	Varies	1% to 3%*	1.0% to 1.5%*
Comments	▸ Can provide help in selecting investment advisers or mutual funds	▸ Can tailor portfolio to individual needs and circumstances ▸ Limited to area of adviser's expertise ▸ Difficult to find comparative information	▸ Extensive comparative information available ▸ Expertise in a broad range of choices ▸ Use no-load or low-load funds to keep costs down

Varies substantially by portfolio size; does not include brokerage commissions

Here are some useful guidelines:
- Use financial planners if you are in need of overall planning advice and coordination among various financial concerns, such as insurance, estate and tax planning, business interests, retirement planning, and long-term savings and investing.
- Investment management expertise—portfolio composition, individual security selection, and buy and sell timing decisions—can be provided by investment advisers (independent counselors, brokerage wrap accounts and bank trust departments) or mutual funds (of which no-load and low-load funds offer the lowest cost.)
- Investment advisers are practical primarily if you have a large portfolio (over $100,000) and want stock selection expertise combined with special portfolio tailoring.
- No-load and low-load mutual funds offer considerable advantages to individual investors regardless of portfolio size, since fees are low, the level of expertise is high and the choice is very broad.
- Individual security selection requires considerable expertise and fairly sizeable portfolios for adequate diversification (at least $25,000 for a diversified stock portfolio). If you do select securities on your own, use mutual funds to help achieve diversification in areas difficult to enter or master (such as foreign markets), and to supplement your individual selections, especially if you have a smaller portfolio.

Implementing Your Plan: Stock Investing Considerations

Implementation of your investment plan means building a portfolio based on the broad outline you have set up.

To the extent that you need growth in your plan, you will be invested in the stock market. Even investors with considerable income needs will most likely be invested in stocks, at least to a small degree.

Whether you use an outside investment adviser, a mutual fund, or simply your own investment skills to invest in the stock market, it is important that you are aware of the overall investment approach that is to be used.

Let's take a closer look at the major overall approaches that should prove to be most useful to an investor.

A Matter of Style

Successful stock investing is not simply a matter of picking stocks willy-nilly, but rather involves an overall investment "style" or "strategy."

Investment style refers to the techniques used to select individual stocks and combining them to form stock portfolios. Investors may have the exact same goals, yet wind up with completely different stocks in their portfolios because they have used different selection criteria. In addition, there are broad timing decisions concerning when to enter or exit the stock market.

Most stock selection strategies tend to fall under two broad categories: technical analysis and fundamental analysis. Timing strategies tend to fall under two categories: market timing and the buy-and-hold approach.

In addition, there is the index fund approach, which is both a stock selection and timing strategy.

The Passive Approach

Actually, the index fund approach is not really a style, but rather no style at all—it is passive investing, because no active investment decisions need to be made. The passive approach consists simply of buying and holding "the market," and it would provide a "market" return less any management and transaction costs; these costs are held to a minimum using this approach. In practice, the passive approach consists of buying and holding stocks that track a market index, the most common of which is the Standard & Poor's 500. However, other market segments can be covered as well—for instance, there are small stock indexes and international indexes that can be used.

This "no style" approach is the benchmark against which any other approach should be measured. An active approach is more expensive, whether it involves your own time and expenses (if you are selecting stocks yourself), or incurs a management fee charged by a mutual fund adviser or private investment adviser. In addition, stocks are usually bought and sold more frequently in an active approach, incurring both transaction costs and taxes on gains.

The index fund approach offers several advantages.

- It is difficult to outperform the overall stock market without added risk.
- Even if it is possible to beat the market, it is difficult for investors to pick in advance an approach that will do so.
- Costs are kept to a minimum.
- Active management can skew a portfolio toward a particular market segment, producing returns that differ from expectations. An index fund that tracks a broad-based index is, by definition, truly diversified. And it is always fully invested in the market.

For any active approach to be useful, it must produce a return above the market rate of return plus the higher costs associated with active management. This higher return represents the value of that approach.

Many investors, of course, feel that it is possible to "beat the market," and use active approaches to add value.

STOCK SELECTION STRATEGIES

Technical analysis is an approach that tries to predict the future price of a stock or the future direction of the stock market based on past price and volume changes. Charts and graphs of stock prices and volume on a periodic basis (daily, weekly, monthly, etc.) are closely examined to detect developing patterns.

The underlying assumption is that stock prices and the stock market follow discernible patterns, and if the beginning of a pattern can be identified, the balance of the pattern can be predicted well enough to yield returns above the market.

Certain technical analysis strategies have proven successful for shorter-term purchase and sell decisions and may be useful in conjunction with an overall fundamental approach. However, most studies indicate that following a solely technical approach as an overall investment strategy does not lead to above-market rates of return.

Fundamental analysis, in contrast, is primarily concerned with the underlying fundamental worth of a firm and its potential for growth. There are studies that indicate certain fundamental analysis techniques can produce above-market rates of return, even when adjusting for risk.

Fundamental analysis can be divided into two camps: growth investing and value investing. Growth investors look for companies with rapid and expanding growth and whose stock prices will grow accordingly with the company's success. Value investors look for companies whose current stock price looks cheap relative to some measure of the firm's real current value, and whose stock price will rise once the market recognizes the firm's real worth.

The growth approach stresses stocks that exhibit above-average and increasing growth in sales and earnings. Growth investors tend to emphasize companies and industries in the stage of rapid and expanding growth in sales and earnings, with still-reasonable profit margins. At a minimum, these companies are usually growing at a rate that is above that of the overall economy. Because they are rapidly growing—and thus plowing earnings back into the firm—dividends, if paid at all, tend to be low.

While this strategy is often associated with smaller, emerging companies, there are larger companies that can be considered "growth" firms, particularly if they are in sectors of the economy that are growing rapidly. In the international arena, the approach can be used on a company basis, as described above, or on a country basis, for instance by investing in countries that are experiencing above-average growth.

Measures associated with this approach typically involve sales growth rates and earnings growth rates, both on an absolute and relative basis. On the other hand, high growth expectations usually involve high stock prices relative to current value—these are expensive stocks, according to the "value" investors' approach.

Growth investing tends to produce investments in more volatile stocks: Prices can move up or down substantially with small changes in expectations or actual earnings performance relative to expected performance.

Value investing puts its emphasis on companies and industries whose market values are low relative to measures of worth based on earnings, dividends or assets. These are often companies that are in unglamorous or out-of-favor businesses—the approach is sometimes referred to as contrarian. However, value investors seek stocks with potential that will eventually be recognized by the market.

Because value stocks tend to be out of favor and prices are relatively low, dividend yields (annual dividend divided by price) tend to be high, but this is not always the case—the approach can be used for investing in smaller firms that may not pay dividends. And it can be used in international investing as well.

Measures associated with this approach include low price-earnings ratios, low price-to-book-value ratios, and high dividend yields.

Value-oriented investing requires patience: It may take considerable time for the market to recognize value, and upturns in company performance may not occur. On the other hand, it tends to be less volatile.

Timing Strategies

There are two basic approaches to the timing question: market timing and buy-and-hold.

A market timing approach involves an attempt to leave the market entirely during downturns and reinvest when the market begins to head back up. Although it is often associated with technical analysis, certain fundamental investors sometimes attempt to time the market—for instance, if they feel the market is overvalued on a fundamental basis.

Buy-and-hold simply means that the portion of your portfolio committed to stocks is fully invested in the stock market at all times. In other words, while you may buy and sell individual stocks, or change to a different mutual fund, your stock portfolio remains invested in the stock market.

If investors could actually enter and leave the market at the right time, it would lead to higher returns. However, there is no satisfactory evidence that market upturns and downturns can be predicted with enough precision to offset the increased transaction costs, not to mention the adverse tax consequences. And if you guess incorrectly, your actual return could be substantially different than expected.

A market-timing approach violates the investment principle concerning time diversification—being invested across different market environments. In general, the longer your holding period, the better.

Possible Strategies

Remember the asset allocation approach described in an earlier chapter? It is possible to go through that process and build an entire stock portfolio using a single approach. For instance, your stock portfolio could consist of an S&P 500 index fund, a small stock index fund, and an international index fund. Or it could consist of a value-oriented large company portion, with smaller commitments to small stocks and international stocks selected using a value-oriented approach, etc.

On the other hand, it isn't necessary to select only one style—in fact, you may be best off diversifying among the active styles. You can also effectively use a combination of active and passive approaches.

One method of doing this is the index-core approach, which uses an index fund for the core portion and actively managed strategies for other segments of the market you want to include.

The core portion should track a broad-based index to ensure a market return. By far the most common is the S&P 500, an index that emphasizes large capitalization companies and represents about 70% of the U.S. stock market. Because of the large number of stocks that must be purchased to track an index, practically speaking, such an approach can only be implemented using an index mutual fund.

The active portion could consist of market segments you want to add for diversification purposes, and that offer opportunities for undiscovered (by the market) value—in other words, areas where an active approach can offer real value. For instance, the market for small stocks, particularly those that are not followed by many analysts, is considered by some to be inefficient and therefore an area where an active approach can add value. Similarly, certain foreign markets are considered "inefficient."

The active portion could also encompass a particular approach you want to emphasize—for instance, a growth-oriented mutual fund you like. Or, it could consist of a stock portfolio that you manage on your own using your own favored strategy. In fact, if you are investing on your own, an index fund is an excellent supplement that assures adequate diversification.

No matter how you implement your investment plan, you should be aware of the investment style. The core approach is merely one possibility for your stock portfolio. Among the various approaches discussed here, there is no one method that has been proven a success under all circumstances. It is largely a matter of which approach, or combination of approaches, makes the most sense to you and fits in with your personal investment profile.

Here are some thoughts to keep in mind:

- The index approach is the lowest cost and will tend to have the lowest tax consequences. There is also less risk that you will not achieve a "market return."
- The value approach will tend to produce higher dividend income than the growth approach (which may be useful if you need some income but also incurs yearly taxes). It will also tend to have lower return volatility.
- The growth approach will tend to have lower dividend income. It will also tend to have higher return volatility (higher risk), with a subsequently higher growth potential.
- Understand that any active strategy runs the risk that you will not achieve a "market" return.
- Stay away from market timing to avoid the risk that you enter or leave the market at a bad time in the economic cycle.

8

Implementing Your Plan: Income Investing Considerations

Most investors seeking income want a relatively assured income flow each year. The income investor's "ideal" portfolio is one that provides a high, stable, and predictable income that doesn't cut into "principal"—that is, the original investment amount. These requirements often lead the income investor to place too much emphasis on yield, and thus to concentrate heavily in fixed-income securities. This emphasis can cause income investors to take on significant risks that they are most likely unaware of.

An understanding of these less well-known risks can help an income investor develop a portfolio that meets real long-term needs.

Understanding Maturity Risks

If you were to survey all of the bonds issued today, one fact would stand out: Higher yields among fixed-income securities are associated with higher credit risks and/or longer maturities. At a given maturity, corporate bonds will have higher yields than government bonds. And for a given credit risk, longer-term bonds will have higher yields than shorter-term bonds.

Credit risk can be reduced significantly through diversification. For instance, the risk that one default will have much impact on a large high-quality corporate bond fund is low.

However, longer-term bonds face more interest rate risk than similar bonds with shorter maturities. Interest rate risk is the risk that a bond's price will drop when interest rates rise, and rise when rates fall. Longer-term bond prices are more volatile than shorter-term bond prices because they have a long future stream of interest payments that don't match the current rates when rates change; the bond price must adjust more to compensate for the change in interest rates.

The only way to reduce interest rate risk among similar bonds is to reduce maturity. This risk can be reduced by diversifying among certain different types of bonds, for instance, high-yield and international bonds. Also, among bonds of similar maturities and credit risk, those that bear higher coupons have less interest rate risk than those bearing lower coupons; their current yields would be similar because the lower coupon bonds would be priced lower than those with higher coupons. Most income investors, though, focus on higher-coupon bonds. And the fact remains that, among bonds of the same type—those with similar credit risks and coupons—longer maturities *always* face greater interest rate risk.

The table below indicates the price variations due to interest rate changes for a 6% coupon bond at various maturities. For instance, if interest rates were to rise by only 1 percentage point, the price of a 6% bond with a one-year maturity would decline only 0.9%, compared to a loss of 4.1% for a five-year bond and a loss of over 12.4% for a 30-year bond.

What if you plan to hold the bond to maturity? You could close your eyes and not look at the change in value—and hope that you don't need to sell before then. You will also have to close your eyes to the higher cash flows paid by newly issued bonds at the time if interest rates rise; your 6% bond may start to wear thin when current bonds are paying 9%.

A Matter of Timing

Another problem with an over-emphasis on yield is one of timing. Longer-term maturity bonds tend to be particularly enticing when the yield differential between long-term and similar short-term securities is particularly large. However, you can see from the table below the risks that go along with seeking higher yield from longer maturities.

For a yield-chasing approach to be successful, the decision to go after the higher yields should be based on your best guess on the future direction of interest rates: If there is a strong chance that they will rise, you would be best off in shorter maturity bonds, so that you can later take advantage of higher yields without a loss of principal.

When is the yield differential likely to be the greatest? Usually this occurs during

Percentage Change in Bond Prices When Interest Rates Change
(for a 6% Coupon Bond)

Years to Maturity	Interest Rates Change by 1%		Interest Rates Change by 2%		Interest Rates Change by 3%	
	Rates Rise	Rates Fall	Rates Rise	Rates Fall	Rates Rise	Rates Fall
1	−0.9%	0.9%	−1.8%	1.9%	−2.8%	2.9%
5	−4.1	4.3	−8.1	8.9	−11.8	13.8
10	−7.1	7.7	−13.5	16.3	−19.5	25.7
15	−9.2	10.4	−17.2	22.4	−24.4	36.0
20	−10.6	12.5	−19.7	27.3	−27.6	44.8
25	−11.7	14.1	−21.4	31.4	−29.6	52.5
30	−12.4	15.4	−22.6	34.7	−30.9	59.9

Investing Basics ...and Beyond

recessions or periods of flat economic growth after rates have dropped significantly—the worst time to make the switch to long-term bonds, since the most likely course is for rates to either remain flat or to start rising. In fact, the reason for the wide yield differential is that the market is predicting higher future rates—and is demanding considerably higher yields on longer-term bonds because of significantly higher risks.

Theoretically, an investor could switch to higher-yielding long-term bonds while rates are flat and switch back just before they start rising. However, if interest rates could be predicted this accurately, there would be more rich economists than there are today.

Don't Forget Stocks

A heavy emphasis on yield and bonds, quite naturally, leads many income investors to forget about stocks. This de-emphasizes growth and exposes the portfolio over time to the possible erosion of real value—as well as real income—due to inflation. Investment approaches that maximize income in the short term tend to inadvertently work toward lowering longer-term portfolio income.

In order to maintain the real level of income in a portfolio, the portfolio must grow enough to offset inflation. However, bonds have no growth element. Instead, that growth must come from stocks. And the less an income investor invests in stocks, the greater his stock portion must grow to overcome inflation.

Let's look at an example to help clarify this dilemma. Let's assume the income yield on

Common Stock Returns Required to Maintain Portfolio Yield

Portfolio Composition			Stock Return Required to Maintain Portfolio Yield (%)			
% in Stocks	% in Bonds	Total Portfolio Yield (%)	3% Inflation	4% Inflation	6% Inflation	8% Inflation
100	0	2.8	5.8	6.8	8.8	10.8
90	10	3.0	6.2	7.2	9.5	11.7
80	20	3.2	6.6	7.8	10.3	12.8
70	30	3.5	7.1	8.5	11.4	14.2
60	40	3.7	7.8	9.5	12.8	16.1
50	50	3.9	8.8	10.8	14.8	18.8
40	60	4.1	10.3	12.8	17.8	22.8
30	70	4.3	12.8	16.1	22.8	29.5
20	80	4.6	17.8	22.8	32.8	42.8
10	90	4.8	32.8	42.8	62.8	82.8
0	100	5.0	—	—	—	—

Shaded area represents unrealistic stock return assumptions.

the S&P 500 index is 2.8%, while the yield on medium-term (five-year maturity) government bonds is 5.0%. A portfolio that is invested 50% in bonds and 50% in the S&P 500 would therefore yield 3.9%.

How can the income provided by this portfolio yield be maintained in real terms if inflation is 3%? The bond portion would not grow at all—it will remain a percentage of a fixed amount. Dividend yield on stocks, however, is a percentage of an increasing amount, so the actual dollars produced rise to help offset inflation. If inflation were 3%, the gain on the common stock portion would have to be at least 6% (3% divided by 50%) for the portfolio to provide a constant real portfolio income. The total return of the stock portfolio—income plus capital gains—would be 8.8% (2.8% + 6%). The total portfolio—50% in bonds and 50% in stocks—would generate an overall total return of 6.9%.

What if the portfolio had less invested in stocks?

The table on the preceding page provides the approximate required return on the common stock portion of the portfolio to maintain a constant total portfolio yield for various compositions and inflation rates. It assumes that dividend and bond yields remain constant at different inflation rates, a strained assumption. However, the table is designed to illustrate the dilemma.

If you emphasize today's yield and thus increase the proportion of bonds, the stock portion diminishes, which means that the remaining common stock portion must provide an even greater return to provide growth to offset inflation.

The shaded portion represents stock return assumptions that are unrealistic in light of historical stock returns—in other words, it would be difficult for an investor to generate these kinds of returns in a common stock portfolio. A diversified portfolio of larger company stocks cannot realistically be expected to generate returns over 12% annually. At high expected inflation rates (6%) and using realistic stock return assumptions, common stocks would have to make up at least 70% of the portfolio to maintain real income in the long term.

Conclusions

If you are an income investor, focusing on the total return of a portfolio over the long term rather than today's yield can help overcome some of these problems.

Remember our "ideal" portfolio for income investors—one that provides a high, stable, and predictable income that doesn't cut into principal? You can reach it by de-emphasizing yield and considering total return and risk:

- Seeking a higher yield is fine as long as you understand the increased risks. If you decide to increase yield by investing in longer-term bonds, make sure you realize the trade-off you are making—you are more at risk for a loss in principal value should interest rates rise.
- If you want a stable and predictable income flow, make sure you take inflation into account. What appears to be "stable" may in fact be a declining amount if it doesn't increase with inflation.

- If you want to fully protect your principal, you must consider inflation risk and the loss it can cause to the real value of your principal.
- You can pick up some extra yield by investing in a large, diversified portfolio of corporate bonds rather than government bonds.
- You can also pick up extra yield by going part way—for instance, by investing at the long end of the short-term spectrum (maturities of one to two years) or in intermediates (up to five years). This also puts you in a better position to safely invest in higher-yielding bonds should interest rates increase.
- Be particularly careful when longer-term rates are most enticing—they are enticing because the risk of rising interest rates is high.
- Don't discount dividend income. A fixed-income yield is a percentage of a fixed amount—your original investment, but a dividend yield is a percentage of a growing amount.
- Make sure that you always keep at least a portion of your portfolio invested in stocks, to provide the growth needed to protect your principal—and real level of income—from inflation.

Keeping these points in mind should help you to develop an ideal income-oriented portfolio that will yield real income—and not unwanted surprises.

9

Fine-Tuning Your Portfolio: Retirement vs. Taxable Investments

At the outset of this book, it was pointed out that the most efficient investment portfolios are based on an overall approach that examines the risk and return potential of your total portfolio, not just the individual parts. That means looking at all of your investable assets as a whole, including those that may be in a retirement account such as an IRA or an employer-sponsored 401(k) plan.

Your total investment portfolio should match your investment profile, which includes your risk tolerance, your return needs, time horizon, and tax exposure. To structure the portfolio, the process starts at the top and works its way down, first allocating among the major asset categories, then within each of those asset categories, and then based on special considerations for certain types of investors. The chapters describing the allocation process centered around discussions of risk, return needs, and time horizon. While ways to reduce the impact of taxes were mentioned, the process at the earlier stages tends to ignore taxes.

Unfortunately, this happy state can't go on forever. You are now at the stage where you can start worrying about taxes—or at least give them some major consideration.

In our current tax structure, "retirement" account is a misnomer. That is, you should not think of your assets as consisting of "retirement" savings and "regular" savings; instead think of your assets as consisting of a tax-deferred portion and a taxable portion.

The question of where you should invest "retirement money" is really a tax-planning decision that is determined after you have decided on the composition of your total investment portfolio. Once you have decided on your portfolio composition, you can then allocate the chosen investments in such a way as to minimize taxes.

At first glance, the decision as to which kinds of investments to allocate to taxable and tax-deferred accounts would appear to be simple: shelter the investments generating the higher amount of annual taxable income, and put those investments that generate gains into taxable accounts.

When it comes to taxes, however, nothing is ever simple.

Any investment with high annual returns—whether they are from income, dividends or realized capital gains—benefits from deferring taxes, and the longer the deferral, the more those benefits are able to compound.

Taxes in tax-deferred accounts are deferred until the assets are withdrawn, at which time they are taxed as income at ordinary income tax rates. In the case of investments with capital gains, the advantage of the lower capital gains tax rate is lost if the asset is placed in a tax-deferred account. However, the advantages of deferring taxes are strong, and when allowed to compound over long time periods—15 to 20 years—they can overwhelm higher tax rates that must be paid on withdrawal for almost all investors other than those who will be in the highest income brackets (36% or above) during retirement.

The best of both worlds, of course, is an investment in which you can defer paying taxes, but which is then taxed at the capital gains rate. This can be accomplished if you hold individual stocks, since you have complete control of the timing decision as to when to sell and realize gains. Many individuals, though, do not hold onto individual stocks for time periods as long as 15 to 20 years.

Most stock mutual funds—even those that have very low portfolio turnover—produce at least some annual distributions. Studies indicate that even low distribution levels on an annual basis tend to tip the scales in favor of tax-deferred accounts for high returning stock mutual funds.

As a rule of thumb, a tax-efficient portfolio is allocated as follows:

- The tax-deferred portion consists of higher-returning investments. Thus, if you hold both stock and bond mutual funds, the stock funds should be allocated to the tax-deferred portion since they tend to produce much higher average annual rates of return, even though bond funds tend to have larger annual distributions. If you hold several kinds of stock funds, those that tend to have higher average annual rates of return should be allocated to the tax-deferred portion—for instance, if you hold both aggressive growth and equity-income funds, the aggressive growth funds should be allocated to the tax-deferred portion, since they tend to produce higher annual returns.
- The taxable portion consists of lower-returning investments, such as balanced funds and bond funds; investments in which you have complete control over the timing decision and that you are likely to hold onto for long time periods, such as long-term individual stock holdings; and investments with built-in tax shelter advantages, such as municipal bonds.

CONCLUSION

Fine-tune your portfolio by making it tax-efficient:

- Try to shelter investments with the highest returns in tax-deferred accounts, such as IRAs and 401(k) plans.
- Investments with lower returns should be relegated to the taxable portion of your portfolio.
- Investments with built-in shelters, such as municipal bonds, and short-term liquid investments that are set aside for emergencies should never be placed in a tax-deferred account.

10

Portfolio Monitoring and Maintenance

Once your portfolio has been constructed and is under way, you should maintain a long-term perspective in your investment program. In terms of your asset allocation scheme, that means sticking with the plan that you have settled on for the long haul.

That doesn't mean, however, that you can ignore your portfolio. First of all, you need to make sure that the portfolio and its various components are performing as planned. And from time to time, you will need to make adjustments to your holdings.

MEASURING PERFORMANCE

A prime concern of most investors is performance: "How well are my investments doing?" You could spend hours calculating various aspects of your portfolio's performance. Let's look at what's really important and why.

First, there is your overall portfolio. Calculating the performance of your total portfolio isn't that difficult if you don't want precision accuracy; the formula is presented on the next page. But is it really necessary to measure the performance of your portfolio as a whole? Measuring the performance of your total portfolio is useful primarily for one reason—to see if the long-term terminal value that you hoped to achieve with your investment program is still realistic.

In general, you should be examining the return on your portfolio to make sure it is within the target range you expected based on your investment mix. If it isn't, you may need to make some adjustments in your future projections—for instance, you may have to increase your savings rate, you may have to take on more risk to achieve the target that you set, or you may simply have to adjust your target value downward, settling for less in the future.

How often need this be done? It really does not need to be done frequently—certainly not more than once a year. Remember you are examining a long-term strategy, and so you need to focus on long-term performance statistics. Don't overcomplicate your life.

Measuring the performance of the various investments that make up your portfolio, on the other hand, should be done much more frequently—either quarterly or semiannually. The purpose of this monitoring is to see how well the professional expertise you have hired (or are performing yourself) is doing.

For instance, you should examine the performance of each mutual fund against its peers (funds with similar objectives) and an appropriate index (an index that covers investments similar to those the fund is investing in) over the same time period. The index and

Calculating Your Return: An Approximation

The equation for an approximate return figure is relatively straightforward:

$$\left[\frac{\text{End Value} + \text{Unreinv. Inc.} - 0.50 \text{ (Net Additions)}}{\text{Beginning Value} + 0.50 \text{ (Net Additions)}} - 1.00 \right] \times 100 = \text{Return (\%)}$$

End Value: *Value at end of investment period.*

Beginning Value: *Value at beginning of investment period.*

Unreinv. Inc.: *Unreinvested income (for instance, dividends or interest received and not reinvested). Note that reinvested income is automatically accounted for because it*

is part of the ending value.

Net Additions: *Total cash additions put into the portfolio during the time period less withdrawals. Use net withdrawals, a negative number, if total withdrawals are greater than total additions.*

peer-average returns provide benchmarks that allow you to better judge the manager's performance. For example, if your fund is up 10% for the quarter and the benchmark index is up 12%, your portfolio manager hasn't really added any value to your investment. On the other hand, if your fund is down 10% while the index is down 15%, your manager has added considerable value—he has limited the loss.

You do not need to make your own calculations to measure the performance of your mutual fund holdings; there are many publications that provide information on mutual fund performance, and that also provide appropriate benchmarks for comparison.

If you are investing in stocks or bonds on your own, measure your individual stock or bond portfolio performance against an appropriate index or similarly managed mutual fund as a test of your own investment decision-making ability. To determine the performance of your own stock portfolio, use the formula above, and make sure that the time period covered is the same as the benchmarks you are comparing the performance against.

If you have an investment adviser selecting individual stocks for you, measure him against an index and mutual fund averages composed of stocks similar to those he is managing. The adviser should be able to provide you with the return on your portfolio; make sure it covers a standard time period, so it can be measured against an index or average that covers the same time period.

What do you do with this performance information? For mutual funds and advisers, if the performance figures are good relative to the benchmarks—no problem. If the figures are unsatisfactory, you have to decide if you want to sell the fund (or drop the adviser) and look elsewhere. Keep in mind that if you sell, you need to find a suitable replacement—one that you feel will do better in the future. And you would not select a fund or an adviser based on only a short-term track record. Similarly, you should not dump a fund or adviser simply because performance has been sub-par short term. While you should examine performance quarterly, don't be overly jumpy if results are poor. Instead, use the opportunity to take a closer look and try to determine why the performance is off; see if you still have confidence in the manager's ability long term.

If you are managing your own stock portfolio, you probably won't want to fire yourself even if performance is off. But you may want to consider revising your overall stock selection strategy. What about evaluation of the performance of individual stocks within your stock portfolio? That should be an ongoing function of your stock selection strategy and not part of your overall portfolio maintenance program.

Portfolio Adjustments

In addition to performance measurement, you also need to review the overall composition of your portfolio and make adjustments when necessary. There are three primary reasons for making adjustments:

- There are changes in your investor profile, which may necessitate an overhaul of your allocation strategy. The changes in your investor profile tend to occur when there are major changes in your life—for instance, when you retire. Or you may simply become more risk-averse. Whatever the case, if any aspect of your investor profile changes, you should go back to the beginning of the process and re-examine your allocation strategy.
- There have been a number of successful investments in the portfolio, and they have become so overweighted that your current investment mix no longer reflects your original plan. For example, your international stock portfolio may have done particularly well over the past few years, and instead of representing 10% of your portfolio, it now represents 18%.
- There are particular investments within the portfolio that are not performing as well as expected, and they may need to be dropped.

When making adjustments to your portfolio, for whatever reason, there are several important considerations to keep in mind.

First, try to avoid tax liabilities. For example, if you need to rebalance your portfolio— for instance, stocks have become overweighted or your profile has changed and you want to de-emphasize stocks—use new money generated from salary, income and capital gains distributions, or from one-time sources such as poorly performing investments, property sales, and inheritances. Investments should be sold because of poor performance, not to rebalance your portfolio. That means that your asset mix may stray several points from the allocation you originally intended. Substitute concerns for minimizing transaction costs and taxes for asset mix precision.

Second, when you are making a major transition from one major investment category to another, do so gradually so that the effects of the market at one point in time don't dramatically affect your portfolio value. For example, if you are moving to a heavier commitment in stocks, don't accomplish this by investing one large lump sum; instead, divide the lump sum up into equal parts and invest it periodically (monthly or quarterly) over a long time period of one or two years; this is known as dollar cost averaging.

Third, a decision to sell an investment can be complicated by tax considerations and the need to find a suitable replacement. Make sure you focus on future return and not on the past. For instance, don't hang on to a mutual fund that has performed badly simply because you want to get back to your original position: If there is an alternative with better return prospects, you will get back to your original position faster in that other fund. Similarly, don't hang on to an investment that has low future prospects simply to avoid taxes.

Conclusion

To keep track of your portfolio over time:

- Measure the performance of your total portfolio every few years to make sure your investment "target" is still within shot.
- Monitor the performance of the components of your portfolio—mutual funds, investment advisers and self-managed investments—either quarterly or semiannually and judge the results against relevant benchmarks.
- Don't make hasty decisions based on short-term performance results.
- When you make adjustments to your portfolio, keep tax liabilities to a minimum—rebalance with new money or proceeds from the sale of investments that perform poorly relative to their investment category. Try to avoid selling assets simply to rebalance.
- When making major adjustments to your portfolio, make the changes gradually over time using dollar cost averaging to reduce the risk that you may be investing at an inopportune time.

Appendix A

Major Reference Sources for Mutual Funds

No-load and low-load mutual funds offer individual investors an excellent means of implementing a well-rounded investment portfolio. The major decision—asset allocation among and within the major categories—must be made by the investor. Once the allocation decisions have been roughed out, it isn't difficult to find mutual funds that fit within the categories described in this book. But the time-consuming and research-intensive process of selecting individual securities and assembling them into a cohesive portfolio can be left to a professional. The following sources can supply you with the information you need to help you in the mutual fund selection process.

AAII PUBLICATIONS

AAII publications are available by sending a note stating the name of the publication and a check to the American Association of Individual Investors, 625 North Michigan Avenue, Chicago, Illinois 60611, or you can charge your order with a Visa or MasterCard by calling (312) 280-0170 or (800) 428-4244 or by fax (312) 280-9833. You can also place orders by sending an E-mail to members@aaii.com or visit our Web site at www.aaii.com.

- *The Individual Investor's Guide to Low-Load Mutual Funds;* this annual publication is free to AAII members and is mailed in March of every year. It covers over 900 low-load mutual funds and includes 10 years of data as well as risk and return performance measures. The price is $24.95 for non-members; additional copies are available to members for $19.
- *Quarterly Low-Load Mutual Fund Update;* this publication is mailed at the beginning of each quarter (January, April, July, and October). It covers over 1,000 low-load mutual funds and provides a summary of fund performance by quarter over the last year and over the most recent three- and five-year periods. The non-member price is $30; $24 for members.
- *AAII.com;* Found under Education in the left-hand menu bar, the Mutual Funds area provides basic articles, a glossary, FAQs, and message board. Use the search tool in this area to find additional articles by going to the Advanced Keyword Search and selecting one of the Mutual Fund options under Category. The Investing Pathways section (found on the right-hand side) has "mini courses," including a Mutual Fund series.

The Tools section (left-hand menu on the home page) includes various resources that can help investors analyze mutual funds, including the Morningstar Mutual Fund Reports, updated quicktake reports on over 10,000 funds provided by Morningstar. The reports contain statistics, as well as analytical tools, rankings, and evaluations. www.aaii.com; free access for members.

OTHER PUBLICATIONS

- *Morningstar Mutual Funds,* Morningstar Inc., 225 W. Wacker Dr., Chicago, Ill. 60606-1228; (800) 735-0700; www.morningstar.com. Published every other week, this service provides full-page reports on 1,700 mutual funds. Each fund page is revised roughly three times a year. This is the mutual fund version of the Value Line stock reports.
- *Morningstar Mutual Fund 500,* Morningstar Inc., 225 W. Wacker Dr., Chicago, Ill. 60606-1228; (800) 735-0700; www.morningstar.com. Published annually, this reference book provides data on 500 mutual funds that Morningstar has identified to be of "exceptional merit."
- *The Value Line Mutual Fund Survey,* 220 East 42nd St., 5th Floor, New York, N.Y. 10017-5891; (800) 634-3583; valueline.com. Published every two weeks, this rivals Morningstar Mutual Funds. It provides full-page analyses on 1,500 mutual funds, with each fund revised roughly three times a year.
- *The Handbook for No-Load Fund Investors,* The No-Load Fund Investor, Inc., 410 Saw Mill River Rd., Ardsley, N.Y., 10502; (800) 252-2042; www.sheldonjacobs.com. This annual publication provides an explanation of how to invest in mutual funds, as well as a directory of no-load and closed-end funds. Tables are used to compare and evaluate mutual fund performance.

Appendix B

Where to Get Information on Outside Investment Expertise

In this book, we have discussed most of the basics you need to know to start building an investment portfolio. However, some individuals would simply prefer to primarily use outside expertise for their investment portfolios. Where do you go to get information, and what kind of information is available?

While there is an enormous amount of information available on mutual funds, it is much more difficult to find information on the other outside experts—financial planners and investment advisers. There is no effective way to "rate" these experts; you must do your own legwork, gathering potential names and researching their backgrounds. In addition, the large number of professional designations can add to the confusion when you are examining their qualifications.

This appendix is primarily devoted to providing sources of information to help ease your legwork.

Financial Planners

Financial planners are generalists who help individuals delineate financial plans with specific objectives, and help coordinate various financial concerns.

Professional designations for the financial planning industry are provided in the table on page 61; sources of information for obtaining lists of financial planners are provided in a table on pages 62 and 63.

What should you look for in a financial planner?
- You will probably want to find a planner that is located close to you, since you will need to spend some time going over your financial concerns.
- Check on the planner's formal educational background, his professional training, and continuing education.
- Make sure you understand the methods of compensation—whether fee-only, or if the planner receives part or all of his compensation through commissions on investment products he sells.
- Most planners will offer free one-hour consultations. Use this opportunity to ask questions and find out if you will get along well with the planner.
- Ask about the make-up of the planner's clientele. You should look for a planner

who is familiar with the kinds of problems you face, and therefore his clientele should have financial situations similar to your own.

- Ask for client references.
- Ask the planner for a copy of his brochure and/or ADV form; the ADV form is filed with the Securities and Exchange Commission and is required if the planner is registered with the SEC. It will disclose an extensive amount of information on the financial planner and his practice, including his philosophies, practice structure, fees, and potential conflicts of interest. If possible, request both Parts I and II. Part II must be provided to clients; Part I is optional, but contains useful information concerning possible past regulatory problems.

INVESTMENT ADVISERS

An investment adviser, or money manager, manages assets, making portfolio composition and individual security selection decisions on a fully discretionary basis. They can range from independent advisory firms to bank trust departments.

Many individuals are amazed to find that it is difficult to get performance information on investment advisers—after all, there are mounds of performance data on mutual funds. However, mutual fund performance can be tracked by independent sources relatively easily by following the fund's net asset value and distributions, both of which are widely reported in the financial press.

In contrast, private money managers have numerous different accounts, sometimes with different individuals responsible for those accounts, and there is no publicly available information on those accounts that would allow for proper performance measurement. Investors who rely on rankings want an indication of how *their* account will be managed, yet there is no guarantee that it will be managed in the same manner as the other accounts. Picking an investment adviser based on performance information is a little like choosing a mutual fund by examining all of the *other* funds in the family except for the fund you want.

Despite these difficulties, there are some publications that provide performance information, and they are listed in the table on pages 62 and 63. There is also a directory of investment advisers, to help you locate one in your area.

When you contact an investment adviser, one of the first questions you will ask, quite naturally, concerns performance.

Remember that the performance information you will receive from a private investment adviser will be generated by the firm itself, although the manager is obligated to disclose relevant details regarding the generation of the performance numbers. Look, in particular, for these details:

- Is the performance a composite of all accounts, or a particular model account? What exactly does it cover?
- Is it net of fees and brokerage commissions?
- Does it cover a standard time period?

Professional Designations: A Guide to the Letters

Financial Planning

CFP (Chartered Financial Planner): Designated by the International Board of Standards and Practices for Certified Financial Planners (based in Denver) to those who complete an approved course, pass a special exam, and meet certain requirements, including work-related experience.

CPA/PFS (Certified Public Accountant/Personal Financial Specialist): Designated by the American Institute of Certified Public Accountants (based in New York) to CPAs who have passed a special exam and meet certain other requirements.

ChFC (Chartered Financial Consultant): Designated by The American College (Bryn Mawr, Pa.) to those who complete a special 10-part course of study and meet certain other professional requirements.

Investment Analysis

CFA (Chartered Financial Analyst): Designated by the Association of Investment Management Research (based in Charlottesville, Va.) to those who pass a rigorous three-level exam (each level of exam must be taken one year apart) administered by the Association covering investment principles, analysis and management, and who meet certain other requirements (including a bachelor's degree or equivalent professional work experience, and three years' experience in investment decision-making).

CIC (Chartered Investment Counselor): Designated by the Investment Counsel Association of America (based in New York) to those holding CFAs who work as investment counselors and meet certain other professional requirements.

Investment Consulting

AIMC (Accredited Investment Management Consultant): Designated by the Institute for Investment Management Consultants (based in Phoenix) to institute members who have completed an investment management consulting course.

CIMC (Certified Investment Management Consultant): Designated by the Institute for Investment Management Consultants (based in Phoenix) to institute members with more professional consulting experience than the AIMC and who meet certain other requirements.

CIMA (Certified Investment Management Analyst): Designated by the Investment Management Consultants Association (based in Denver) to those who have passed a one-week course of study at Wharton and a special exam, and who meet certain other professional requirements.

- Does it reflect accounts similar to your own in size and strategy?

Other items to look for in an investment adviser are:

- Make sure you understand the adviser's investment strategy. It should be clearly defined, and conform to your own needs and circumstances.
- Make sure that the performance numbers you have examined were generated by individuals who will be managing your portfolio.
- Find out if your account will be individually tailored, or part of an investment pool.
- Check references: Speak with clients who have been with the manager over

various periods of time.

- An audit from a CPA firm adds a degree of comfort to the performance statistics, but there are no industry standards for audits of money managers' track records.
- Ask for Form ADV, which registered investment advisers are required to file annually with the SEC. Part II of this document must be provided to prospective investors, although many only provide it on request. This part covers fees, strategies used by the firm, type of clients, and in-depth profiles of the firm's principals. It is not necessary for managers to provide Part I, which tells you if any of the principals have had legal or regulatory problems in the past, or may have potential conflicts of interest. Obviously, it would be nice to review the full form.

Where to Go

Financial Planners

Below are professional organizations that will provide lists of financial planners in your area and other information:

American Institute of CPAs
888/777-7077
www.aicpa.org
Will provide a list of CPA/PFS financial planners.

Certified Financial Planner Board of Standards
888/237-6275
www.cfp-board.org
Will indicate whether a financial planner has passed the CFP and is still in good standing.

Financial Planning Association
800/322-4237
www.fpanet.org
Will provide information on financial planners in a specified location who have the CFP designation.

National Association of Personal Financial Advisors
888/333-6659
www.napfa.org
Will provide a list of fee-only financial planners.

Investment Advisers

The following publications cover registered investment advisers although several are geared toward the institutional (pension fund and endowments) industry and include managers with account minimums over $1 million. They are all available for purchase, but some may also be found in public and business school libraries.

Money Manager Review
1550 California St., Suite 263
San Francisco, Calif. 94109
415/386-7111
www.managerreview.com
The firm tracks about 800 investment advisers based on performance information supplied by the advisers; the Review publishes information on the top 15%. Managers are compared within their own risk groups; the reports section provides half-page write-ups on the individual managers covered. Price: $295/year.

Nelson's Directory of Investment Managers
Nelson Information
One Gateway Plaza
Port Chester, N.Y. 10573
914/937-8400
www.nelnet.com
Provides a listing of over 2,000 advisers who actively manage

Investment Consultants

The difficulty in evaluating investment adviser performance has led to a whole new field of professionals who specialize in just that—helping investors evaluate advisers. Many investment consultants specialize in evaluations for large institutions, such as pension plans, where the compensation can be high. Other consultants, however, do help individuals evaluate, select and monitor investment advisers. Among these are independent consulting firms and brokerage firms, which offer manager selection services using wrap accounts. In fact, among brokerage firms, investment consulting is one of the major areas of growth.

The table on page 61 and the one below provide professional designations for the

More Information

assets on a fully discretionary basis; focuses primarily on advisers with large minimums who handle institutional (pension plan) assets. Most listings include annual return data based on information supplied by the managers. Price: $595.

Directory of Registered Investment Advisors
Standard and Poor's Money Market Directories
320 E. Main St., P.O. Box 1608
Charlottesville, Va. 22902
800/446-2810
www.mmdaccess.com
Directory includes over 13,000 SEC-registered firms listed by state. The criteria for listing is SEC registration, so the book includes some firms that do not necessarily manage money (such as newsletters, financial planners and stockbrokers). No performance data is included. Price: $460.

Investment Consultants

Listed below are professional organizations that will provide select lists of investment consultants in your area:

Institute for Certified Investment Management Consultants
202/452-8670
www.icimc.org

Will provide a list of investment consultants with the AIMC or CIMC designation.

Investment Management Consultants Association
303/770-3377
www.imca.org
Will provide a list of investment consultants with the CIMA designation.

investment consulting industry, as well as sources of information for obtaining lists of consultants.

What should you look for in a consultant?

- Make sure you understand how the consulting firm is compensated and if there are any affiliates the firm is involved with. Typically, investment consulting firms will fall into one of three categories: they may be affiliated with a brokerage firm, they may be an independent firm with a brokerage affiliate, or they may be an insurance company subsidiary. Compensation may be through fees, commissions, or a combination. Check to see if the fees are paid by you, and if there are commission dollars that are directed by the money management firms being recommended.
- Ask if the consulting firm provides and/or sells information to advisers. Do the advisers in the database have to pay or purchase data from the consultant to be included in the database?
- Find out how the information in the consulting firm's database is compiled and verified.
- Ask if the firm personally interviews the advisers evaluated. How many advisers in the database have been evaluated in face-to-face interviews?
- Check the professional background of the consultant, including professional associations.
- Look for consultants who handle clients that are in financial circumstances similar to your own.

While selecting an outside expert may be easier than doing all your own work, it isn't Easy Street. However, these sources of information should lighten the load.

Appendix C

Where to Learn More About Investing

There are many good textbooks that go into considerable detail about stocks, bonds, and the market environment. These books, for instance, will discuss in great detail the various kinds of stocks and bonds, stock and bond quotations, how the overall economy may affect various securities, how to analyze stocks, etc.

   Listed below are some textbooks you may find useful if you want to learn more about investing fundamentals.

INVESTMENT TEXTBOOKS

Listed in order of difficulty, from beginning-level to more advanced.

- Hirt, Geoffrey A. and Stanley B. Block; *Fundamentals of Investment Management,* sixth edition; McGraw-Hill, Inc., New York, N.Y., 1998. A very understandable and well-written book for the novice. Numerous examples and excellent references for sources of investment information.
- Gitman, Lawrence J. and Michael D. Joehnk, *Fundamentals of Investing,* seventh edition, Addison-Wesley, Boston, Mass., 1999. Understandable and well-written, with a focus on portfolios and strategies for implementing investment goals in light of risk/return trade-offs.
- Cohen, Jerome B., Edward D. Zinbarg, and Arthur Zeikel; *Investment Analysis and Portfolio Management,* fifth edition; McGraw-Hill, Inc., New York, N.Y., 1987. One of the best books on investment management.

TWO CLASSICS

- Graham, Benjamin; *The Intelligent Investor,* fourth edition; HarperCollins, New York, 1997. A version of *Security Analysis* (below), written for the individual investor (vs. the professional).
- Cottle, Sidney, Roger F. Murray, and Frank E. Block; *Graham and Dodd's Security Analysis,* fifth edition; McGraw-Hill Inc., New York, 1996. One of the most important books for the security analyst. Discusses the behavior of the securities markets, balance sheet analysis, interpretation of financial data, specific standards for bond investment, techniques of selecting stocks for investment, projections of earnings and dividends, methods for valuing growth stocks, and stock-option

warrants. This is an update of the classic *Security Analysis: Principles and Techniques* by Benjamin Graham, David Dodd, and Sidney Cottle, which introduced the valuation approach to security analysis.